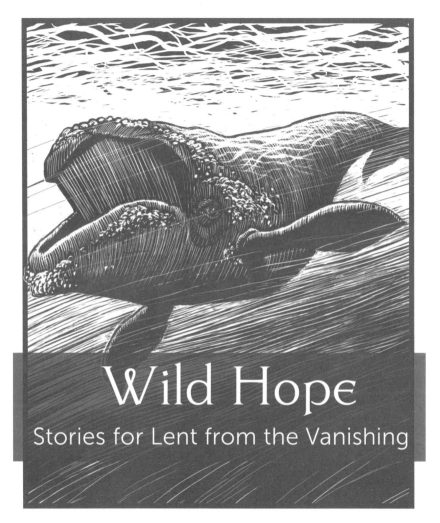

Wild Hope

Stories for Lent from the Vanishing

GAYLE BOSS
ILLUSTRATED BY DAVID G. KLEIN

PARACLETE PRESS
BREWSTER, MASSACHUSETTS

For the scientists and conservationists
devoted to Earth's wild creatures

———◦◦◦◦———

2020 First Printing

Wild Hope: Stories for Lent from the Vanishing

Text copyright © 2020 by Gayle Boss
Illustrations copyright © 2020 by David G. Klein

ISBN 978-1-64060-199-4

The Paraclete Press name and logo (dove on cross) are trademarks of Paraclete Press, Inc.

Library of Congress Cataloging-in-Publication Data
Names: Boss, Gayle, author. | Klein, David G., illustrator.
Title: Wild hope : stories for Lent from the vanishing / Gayle Boss ;
   Illustrated by David G. Klein.
Description: Brewster, Massachusetts : Paraclete Press, 2020. | Includes
   bibliographical references. | Summary: "Illustrated stories of the
   world's magnificent, intricate, and vanishing creatures with the
   resurrection hope of rebirth"— Provided by publisher.
Identifiers: LCCN 2019044903 | ISBN 9781640601994 (trade paperback) | ISBN
   9781640604377 (mobi) | ISBN 9781640604384 (epub) | ISBN 9781640604391(pdf)
Subjects: LCSH: Animals—Religious aspects—Christianity—Juvenile
   literature. | Extinct animals—Juvenile literature. |
   Resurrection—Meditations—Juvenile literature. |
   Lent—Miscellanea—Meditations—Juvenile literature.
Classification: LCC BT746 .B67 2020 | DDC 242/.34—dc23

LC record available at https://lccn.loc.gov/2019044903

10 9 8 7 6 5 4 3 2 1

Published by Paraclete Press
Brewster, Massachusetts
www.paracletepress.com

Printed in Canada

CONTENTS

INTRODUCTION

All creation groans in this one great act of giving birth.
Romans 8:22*

"Look," I said, index finger tapping a dictionary entry, "'Lent,' in its root word, means 'spring.'" My two young sons glanced out the window at the snow-covered yard. "That means Lent is a time for us, like other living things in spring, to grow." The older boy nodded dutifully. The younger asked if he could have a cookie.

Those two boys are adults now. In all the years they sat at our table, I never found a way to talk about Lent that made their faces light up and their limbs twitch with intrigue. Little wonder, since I had no affection for the season. Lent meant pained self-examination and fervent scouring of the internal house—fervency that faded as the season wore on.

One year I thought I'd found the way to enliven Lent. I learned that for centuries the church had pointed to Noah's Ark as a symbol of "our Lenten passage." Ah, a story—featuring a boat massively bigger than Grandpa's! And animals, which never failed to get the boys' attention. I dug out a basket for our ark. The small model animals already in the toy box, plus some new ones they eagerly picked out at the bookstore, would be the ark's lucky occupants. Each night after supper one of the boys would choose an animal he wanted to put in the basket-ark and tell what he liked about that animal, why he was glad to have it onboard: the amazing speed of the cheetah, the amazing acrobatics of the monkey, the eagle's amazing eye. . . .

They were attentive, I was engaged. Next, the spiritual application: Noah's story is our story, I told the boys. The ark is the church, the community that carries us

---

* This is the translation by Fr. Richard Rohr in his book *The Universal Christ: How a Forgotten Reality Can Change Everything We See, Hope For, and Believe* (New York: Convergent, 2019), 96.

across the roiling chaos of our lives—personal troubles and public troubles. All that water—it's the chaos, and also the water of baptism that strips off the tough husk we wear so that love can spill out of us.

I watched my sons' faces go blank, their bodies slump in their chairs. They wanted to talk about the ark's screeching, leaping, hissing, slithering animals. Alas, the church gave no instruction on the animals' symbolic value. The animals were merely animals.

All of this was before the words "climate change" and "mass extinction" floated in our shared cultural air. Biologists now tell us that Earth is undergoing its sixth mass extinction—species loss is that rapid. The first five extinctions spiraled out of geologic cataclysms of one kind or another—an asteroid-Earth collision, tectonic-plate shift, volcanic eruption. Today's cataclysm is a new kind. For the past century, whole species have been disappearing a hundred times faster, by conservative estimates, than in the past, because the choices about shelter, food, transportation, communication, and leisure that we humans make every day are pounding the planet. We are laying waste the animals' only home.

Which is the only home of human animals too. This beautiful blue-green globe is the one ark we all ride.

The boys had it right all along. Attention to the amazingness of our arkmates routes us directly to the heart of Lent. The season means to rouse us from our self-absorption. Absorbed instead in the beauty of other creatures, we see how they value their lives, lives woven together across species in beautifully complex webs. The nine-ounce red knot flies from the southern tip of the world to meet the horseshoe crab at precisely the week she crawls from the waters of Delaware Bay to lay her eggs. Once alive to the exquisite web holding all creatures, we also see the holes slashed through it. By us. We're enraptured by the animals' beauty, and we're horrified by the suffering we inflict on that beauty. With Saint Paul we can hear all creation groaning,[†] including ourselves.

---

† See Romans 8:22, quoted above.

I didn't hear all creation groaning when my sons were young. I was oblivious to the millions dying, their kinds never to be seen on the earth again. If I had known, I wonder if I would have been able to tell the boys. They had not yet learned to feel themselves separate from any living thing, a separation we adults find necessary to function efficiently. Probably they would have cried. Or maybe, in rage, thrown things. Certainly they'd have been confused about the Creator who, I told them, cared for the falling of the smallest sparrow. Sad, angry, confused, they would have suffered with the suffering of God's beauty. Which would have brought us to the white-hot core of Lent.

Not a place I want to go, much less bring children to. But a place I now can't avoid.

———⊱•⊰———

The first Christmas my sons were both in their twenties, I was at my childhood home and noticed the new issue of *National Geographic.* Riffling through it, I saw a feature story on those great orange apes, orangutans. A quick glance at the pictures told me this was not a story that would enhance holiday cheer. I put the magazine at the bottom of the pile and tried to forget about it. But one of the pictures—eight baby orangutans in a wheelbarrow—kept swimming into my mind. A month later, I gave in. I found the magazine and read the story. A few days later a friend gave me an article from *Audubon* magazine about the amazing, imperiled red knot.

The global wave of animal suffering caught me up. It has indeed taken me to the white-hot core of Lent where I've felt broken open and sick at the revelation that the way we live is, each year, killing millions of magnificent, innocent creatures of all kinds. I've had to see and confess that my habits of body, mind, and heart aid the slaughter of God's beauty.

Two thousand years ago, long before the current extinction crisis, Saint Paul heard all creatures groaning. We human creatures are groaning, he said, because we've had some glimpse of who we might be, and it's painful to wait for our full transformation into persons of unbounded love and compassion. Other creatures, already fully themselves, groan in the pain that humans inflict on them. They suffer sacrificially, because of and for us. If we'll hear them groaning, they'll midwife our birth into new lives of unbounded compassion—what Paul called "the glorious liberty of the children of God." Then our freedom will be their freedom.‡

The stories that follow are of animals groaning at the brink of extinction. The nonhuman animals described are suffering the pain of impending death. They too are the hungry, the homeless, the hunted of the earth—"the least of these," Christ's brothers and sisters.§ The human animals described suffer with them. Born into a larger compassion, these people see turtles and birds, apes, insects, fish, and amphibians as kin. They also suffer knowing that the animals' peril foreshadows our own.

For this format, I've had to greatly simplify both the miracle and the peril of each creature. And I've had to leave the stories of thousands of equally magnificent and endangered animals untold. These few serve here as messengers for the many. They can alert us to the precarious and pregnant moment we're in. The purpose of Lent has always been to startle us awake to the true state of our hearts and the world we've made. Which wakes an aching, wild hope that something new might be born of the ruin.

The promise of Lent is that something *will* be born of the ruin, something so astoundingly better than the present moment that we cannot imagine it. Lent is seeded with resurrection. The Resurrection promises that a new future will be given to us when we beg to be stripped of the lie of separation, when the hard husk suffocating our hearts breaks open and, like children again, we feel the suffering of any creature as our own. That this can happen is the wild, not impossible hope of all creation.

‡ See Romans 8:19–32, Revised Standard Version (RSV).
§ See Matthew 25:40, New International Version (NIV).

If I had it to do again, I would tell my young sons about the suffering and deaths of the amazing animals they love. I would let their hearts be broken. Then I would tell them that hearts broken open in love create a new ark. That when we suffer in love together, a Suffering Love beyond us can birth, through us, a new world where "they will not hurt or destroy in all my holy mountain."[||] This is what we and all creatures groan for—this more beautiful world that lies quietly waiting in every heart.

HOW TO USE THIS BOOK

For each week of Lent there are stories of four animals. In weeks one through five, the stories can be read on any days of the week. In week six, Holy Week, the reading days are specified.

[||] See Isaiah 11:9, Revised Standard Version (RSV).

Sumatran Orangutan

Balanced on his mother's hip high above the rainforest floor, the baby stares at her mouth, rapt. A pencil-size twig she's peeled smooth hangs between her lips. She pokes the twig into the fruit of a neesia tree she holds with both hands, working her lips so that it scours stinging hairs off the seeds inside and wiggles them loose. Then she takes the tool from her lips and shakes the seeds into her mouth. The baby reaches up a crooked finger and pulls back her lower lip, the better to watch her teeth strip the coats—rich in fat—from the seeds. The seeds themselves she spits out, moving for a moment his inquisitive finger.

Two years old and carried everywhere, the little one is learning every moment all things orangutan. There are a lot of them. So many, in fact, that his mother will lavish her attention on him, teaching him for eight years before birthing another child. Watching them, the humans of this place gave them the name *orang-hutan*, "person of the forest."

Thirsty, the mother orang stands and tips her body—baby wide eyed and clinging—into space. She catches a branch, then swings to another, and another, the sound like a rustling of colossal skirts. Arriving at a tree she knows has deep holes where water collects, she pulls off a branch, dips it into a hole, draws it out, and squeezes the wet leaves, dribbling water into her mouth. Then she sprinkles the babe's upturned face.

The mother learned this from her mother and others she's watched in her forty-five years in the treetops. Also, how to use leaves as an umbrella, as gloves, and a pillow. Though orangutans don't live in social groups like other apes, they pass on ingenious innovations. They create an orangutan culture unique to their locale—locales now cut off from each other.

A century ago, a hundred thousand of this species swung through the canopy from one end of the Indonesian island of Sumatra to the other. Now confined to nine pockets of forest at the island's northern tip, they number fewer than seven thousand. And hundreds are lost every year.

With a full stomach and midday heat building, the mother hoists her babe onto her back and swishes to a tree suitable for her next purpose. Braced against the trunk, she yanks branches into her lap. The little one, peering over her shoulder, watches her long, deft fingers expertly weave them into a nest. Every day she makes two—a siesta nest and a nighttime nest. Finished, it's sturdy enough to hold her nearly one hundred pounds, and the baby, and another. Because it's likely, at nap time, for her older son to join them. Now ten, he's beginning to live on his own, but for two years yet he'll return often to his mother for her food offerings, lessons in tool use, and comfort.

This afternoon he's the first to wake and pull away from the soft knot of their bodies. Usually he waits for his mother to rouse and nurse the baby. Then, after they swing away, he might take the nest apart, examining his mother's construction. Today he stretches tall on an adjacent limb, nostrils working. Soon his mother joins him, baby clasped across her chest.

Smoke seeps through the canopy, an acrid fog. The young male is already rubbing his eyes. Mother leading, they begin to climb, trying to get above the sting and choke. But smoke climbs faster. In the distance, they catch glimpses of leaping orange tongues.

The trees have been cut and fire set to the ruin—preparation for another plantation of oil palm trees. Cookies, ice cream, cake mixes and chocolate, bagged bread and pizza dough, lotions, lipstick, toothpaste, soaps, shampoo—half the packaged products in supermarkets are made with oil pressed from the trees' fruit. It's versatile and cheap. Palm oil corporations can't keep up with demand, not even after felling and burning tens of millions of acres of humming, lush rainforest that is the only home of orangutans, and thousands of other species.

In another pocket of rainforest a hundred miles away, in a small building, two women bottle-feed baby orangutans. Outside, three men carry youngsters, a little older, to wheelbarrows for a field trip—climbing lessons in the trees. Six or seven to a barrow, they hold to each other as they would to their mothers. The only way to separate a mother orangutan from her child is to kill her. It's the usual solution when she is found wandering in oil palm plantations, hungry, after her home trees have been burned. The babies, faces rippling with emotion, reach for a body, any body, to hold. Poorly paid plantation workers can sell them for high prices to people who want to hold them as pets. The lucky ones are found and brought to this care center where other people do their best to mother them into orangutans who can survive in the forest that remains.

One substitute mother bends over a crib to photograph a refugee orphan, who reaches for her camera. *Yes, little one,* the woman says, *this also may be a tool of your survival.* She posts online the portraits of the babies she cares for, hoping those who see them say, *Oh, they look so much like ours!* She hopes they'll see these "persons of the forest" as, yes, persons.

WEEK ONE

The Hungry

Red Knot

Shoulder to shoulder, hundreds of stout little birds pace the edge of the ebbing tide. All at once they burst up. Then flutter down, regroup, pace again.

It's an evening in late February, and everything in them tells the flock of red knots, *Leave, soon.* They're synchronizing a pole-to-pole flight precisely with the movements of creatures a continent away. As with aerial acrobats, a gap in connections is apt to be fatal.

For almost five months they've been preparing themselves for this feat. Last October they dropped onto this thumb of land at the southern end of the earth famished, having spent every last coin of strength flying 9,500 miles from the Canadian Arctic—after they'd labored to hatch and fledge a clutch of chicks on the unforgiving tundra. Through blinding gales they've probed the tidal plain of Tierra del Fuego, gobbling little clams and mussels whole. They've kept their intention singular: to regain weight and rebuild breast muscle. Their return trip, not a mile shorter, will perhaps cost them more. Now the weight of an avocado, they preen the new set of flight feathers they've grown for this moment. Ready, sensing the tick of their internal clocks, still they wait for better weather. Stiff winds and storms sap precious reserves and skew their impeccable timing.

Finally, a clear, calm window opens in the evening sky. With a shuddering *swoosh* they lift and wheel, curving smoothly, sinuously upward, upward, one bird never jostling another, one vast, winged body.

Up the South American coast they'll hop, aiming for beaches of northern Brazil. Arriving in April, they're half an avocado's heft. And brighter. Along the way gray and white feathers on their heads and breasts began to molt and grow in a warm cinnamon. These are the feathers that name the knots "red" and attract mates eight weeks hence. As their breeding plumage fills in, the birds scour these tidal flats, avid to refuel for the journey's next, most precarious leg. But each year there are fewer and smaller shellfish in the warmer, more acidic ocean. Each year the knots must work harder to regain the weight lost getting here. Some won't.

The flock stays and feeds as long as it dares. But its appointment with an ancient creature farther up the Atlantic insists. So on an early May evening they rise again, white bellies gleaming in the twilight. They climb to twenty thousand feet, stroking above the open ocean, guided only by the stars and motions of the sun, three days, four days—barring hurricanes—no food, no water, calling a soft *knupp-knupp* to each other across the thin air.

If all is as it should be, the knots will slide down the last of 3,500 miles and land on the beaches of Delaware Bay just as horseshoe crabs are rowing back out to sea. With the full and new moons of May the crabs swim ashore and spawn, leaving billions of green eggs the size of pinheads. Ravenous, emaciated, the birds pump their bills up and down in the sand like sewing-machine needles. Most of the world's red knots are here, now. Nowhere else and at no other time is their table laid with these tiny gems of pure energy.

And just when they need them. Though the little birds have flown 7,500 miles from Tierra del Fuego, 2,000 more stretch ahead—and then the intensity of mating, laying, hatching, and defending chicks on the Arctic tundra. To be ready, each one labors to double its weight again, which means swallowing four hundred thousand little green eggs in about twelve days. Because the knots have an appointment with lives in the Arctic too. There, during a narrow slice of June, insects will hatch—food for the chicks that must also be hatched by then. The knots must leave Delaware Bay by the end of May, or the offspring they've not yet conceived will break from their eggs into air empty of insect larvae and starve.

On the month's last day, one bird rests in a woman's hand. She can feel his heart flutter within his too-narrow breast. Like many of the knots her team has weighed, measured, and banded, he has not eaten anywhere near his egg quota. For years, fishermen took too many crabs from the bay. Plus, a roiling storm—of which there are more as water and air currents around the globe warm—confused the spawning schedule of the crabs that are left. And storm surge stole the bit of unbuilt beach where these expected to bury their eggs. All that loss means this little bird is apt to be lost too. Seventy-five percent of the world's red knots have been lost in the woman's lifetime.

It's why she's come. She and her team have synchronized their lives with those of the knot. All along the flyway they count, measure, and monitor—from the size of South American shellfish to the number of Arctic nests. With tens of thousands of data points they paint pictures of wonder and loss for all of us. *See this palmful of bird,* the woman says, *see his magnificent endurance and resilience—all of it evoked for exquisite timing. Imagine living exquisitely intertwined with creatures worlds away. What might be evoked in us?*

Kneeling in the sand the woman presses her cheek against the quiet bird's soft wing and breathes what she wants to be strength, and is surely love, into his neck. Then opens her hand.

Amur Leopard

Thin indigo light softens the boreal forest at dusk. She settles on a rocky outcrop and pieces her creamy winter coat, studded with black rosettes, into the patchwork of snow, shadow, rock, bark. Seamless. Even her quick whiskers still their twitch. She slits her gray-green eyes against the insistent wind and peers into the forest below for roe deer, sika deer—or tigers. Finding no opportunity, no threat, she glides to a ledge tucked in under the outcrop. She lifts her head and coughs. The mottled rock-shadow-bark behind the outcrop breaks apart and three nearly grown cubs tumble toward her call.

Three! the men exclaim. They replay the video again and again. Their camera traps first caught the leopard family a year ago when the cubs were six months old, but, elusive as ghosts, they've evaded the lens since. On their screen the men see the mother tear meat from the deer carcass she's hidden on the ledge. When the cubs arrive she moves aside and the largest charges the carcass. The two smaller cubs fidget at a respectful distance, licking their lips while he feasts and purrs. The next largest gets her turn at the meat, but just as she, full bellied, loses interest, the mother lurches up, eyes fixed and glowing. Her bark-cough commands *Run*. The smallest cub goes hungry, again.

She is scrappy, though, and now over a year-and-a-half old she will likely live to birth her own young. The men are proud of her, and even more proud of her mother. Though a litter of three is not rare, few leopardesses can feed and protect more than two cubs to adulthood. This fierce mother is one such. The men recognize her by the pattern of her rosettes, singular as a fingerprint. They knew her as a cub with her mother. They knew her grandmother too, one of the first big cats they identified with camera traps. Before camera traps, they skied the forests for weeks, sleeping under spruce trees, studying tracks in the snow to know how many Amur leopards were left in Russia's Far East.

About thirty, the first counters estimated in 1972. They'd surveyed the swath of the Amur River basin in southeastern Russia, northeastern China, and the Korean peninsula where the leopards thrived for millennia. A master of adaptation, a cat that appeared on Earth south of Africa's Sahara reshaped itself—thicker fur and tail, lighter torso, limbs longer for snow-walking—to flourish in the harsh taiga. Until humans arrived with guns, fire, and heavy machinery. Of thousands, thirty leopards survived, backed into a thin slice of Primorsky Province. "A classic extinction pattern," researchers noted, preparing their hearts for Amur leopard absence.

Yet thirty, plus or minus a few, persisted for decades. Confounded, elated, desperate, Russian conservationists and international partners lobbied the Russian government to give back to Amur leopards a portion of their home forests. In 2012, it did, opening Land of the Leopard National Park. In an area about one-third of the size of Yellowstone, four hundred cameras watch the forest. Protected, the leopards have tripled their numbers, again astounding scientists, who predicted the parkland could support no more than a doubling.

In late spring, the fierce mother leaves her cubs. Fully grown, they must now be fully leopard. Solitary. The two females settle into territory near their mother's. But male leopards claim home ranges about three times the size of females' ranges, and in this part of the forest that claim has been laid by a large male who strictly enforces it.

The young male turns north. As he passes along ridgetops and through valleys, resident males warn him not to linger. Mid-summer he reaches the park's northern border. It means nothing to him. His singular drive is to find a breeding and hunting ground not guarded by another. He cannot know that across this border there are humans who regard the hunting ground as solely their own. For generations they hunted deer without limit. The leopards that didn't starve, these hunters killed as competitors, with the bonus that people near and far paid them handsomely for the great cats' luxurious fur coats and medicinal bones.

There are legal limits on deer kills now. But generational lifeways evolve slowly.

The young male pads across the park border and finds land not marked by another cat. Crouched on a ridge one autumn evening, he sits suddenly upright. Sharp, clanging sounds drive sika deer galloping toward him. His body jerks to chase—his body jerks to flee. Fear wins. He sprints, springs across a chasm, and comes, panting, to a rise. Below he sees men banging pots to terrify deer toward men with guns.

He's on the move again. If he escapes hunters, he's apt to run into walls of fire farmers set each fall and spring to stimulate the growth of hayfields they've cut out of wild forests. Hungry, he may leap the fences of their livestock pens, which they guard with guns.

No camera records this. But using the footage of his earlier life with his mother and sisters, Russian researchers made a reality TV show. *Spotted Family* riveted viewers. Now celebrities, politicians, and school soccer teams "sponsor" leopards in the national park. They insist that police enforce protections. And across the park's western border in China, conservationists have persuaded their government to create a national park adjoining Russia's that expands by six times the land protected for far-ranging big cats.

Winter comes early to the taiga. Trying to go farther north, the young male curls against a sudden blizzard. He beds beneath a spruce. Then a resilience bred over millennia rouses him. He shakes, sniffs the wind, and pushes on.

Galapagos Penguin

Deep beneath the surface of the Pacific Ocean a barrel-chested current carrying a thousand times more water than the Mississippi River pushes eastward along the equator—until, six hundred miles shy of Ecuador, it hits a wall. Magma erupting from the ocean floor a million years ago cooled into an island smack in the current's path. Forced to the surface and sunlight, the nutrient-rich waters bloomed, setting off an evolutionary food chain reaction full of surprises.

Penguins, for instance, diminutive ones. One-tenth the weight of their Emperor cousins, they stand on the volcanic rock hunched over their unfeathered feet, shading them from the tropical sun. Not all penguins live in ice and snow, but of the eighteen species, only the Galapagos penguin dares the equator.

Though July is a cooler month on Isabela, largest of the Galapagos Islands, still the penguins pant. Suddenly the bay begins to boil. Dolphins have herded a school of mullet in from deeper waters. The penguins speed-waddle to the sea's edge and fling themselves into the silver cyclone, diving, flying together through the water sleek and quick, a synchronized swim to pen the mullet, then snatch them from beneath. From above, a dive-bombing pelican pierces the swarm. He scoops up so many fish, he finds his weighted bill too heavy to lift. Forced to open it a crack to drain water from his catch, he lets a few mullet escape—and flinches as the penguins rocket in to snatch them clean from his pouch's lip. Blue-footed boobies dive in too, and brown noddies hover at the surface, picking off mullet stragglers until the plate of the bay is clean.

It's been a good month for these communal feeding frenzies. The mighty Equatorial Undercurrent has surged up strong and cool, thickening the waters along Isabela's west coast with algae-eating plankton and zooplankton. Mullet, sardines, and anchovies are quick to find the plankton banquet, and when they do, penguins and other piscivores are right behind them, gorging. But there's no telling when feast will shrivel to famine.

Most of the penguins leave this year's fish-full waters by August. Fat, they hunch on shore or hide from the heat in rock crevices while their feathers fall out. The equatorial sun bakes their feathers brittle faster than the sun shining on penguins in other places. Not once, like their cousins, but twice a year Galapagos penguins must grow a whole new tuxedo. They want to be fat beneath the old suit when it falls away. Because fishing in cold water wearing scanty feathers is too energy costly, they fast while they molt. After fifteen days they're well feathered again—and thin.

They scramble to the sea. In the absence of a fish boil, they gulp any small swimmers they find and weigh survival options. Having lived through the molting-fast, each one asks, *Can I re-fatten enough for the exertions of mating and parenting?* It's a risk hinged on fish supply, which hinges on the strength of the cold upwelling current, which hinges on climate forces as massive as the planet.

Clambering across the rock, a scientist smiles to see males flipper-patting females and braying like donkeys. Because the water's temperature is cool, she expects this—penguins mating, taking the risk of chicks. She kneels and slides her gloved hand into a nest-crevice she's visited before. Yes, a bird within, a male she banded several mating seasons ago. Camped among the docile birds for the first time fifty years ago, she observed that individuals have unique facial markings and breast freckles. No one had known that—or much else about these creatures—before her 1970 field study.

She weighs the nesting male: over five pounds! If his mate is equally fat, and if the cold-water upwelling continues, this pair may be able to raise both of their eggs to fledging chicks—an occasion to celebrate. A year ago, when the bay tested ten Fahrenheit degrees warmer, she found not a single nest or egg. Every daylight hour the penguins foraged the fish-sparse waters and still met her on shore at evening thin and worn. Some collapsed during the molt. Survivors showed no interest in mating. To sit on eggs instead of searching for fish would invite starvation, both for themselves and for any chick that might hatch.

But this year the current has delivered cool waters, and these penguins—flexible enough to breed in any month, waiting till the eating's good—are busy trying to recoup last year's losses.

The scientist watches the sleek male settle again on his eggs. Sighing, she realizes she had steeled herself for the scene she came upon in 1972, and again in 1998: emaciated birds slicked green. A very strong El Niño had weakened the Equatorial Undercurrent and the shallower Peru Current, suppressing any upwellings of cold, fish-rich water around Isabela. Though the penguins spent all day in the algae-clogged water, they found little to eat. After another such event in 1982–83, researchers counted 65 percent fewer birds. Somehow in last year's strong El Niño more of them held on.

It gives her hope, but she knows the trend. Even in this good year she counts half the number of penguins she counted in 1970. "Super El Niños" have become more frequent in the past century; some climate models predict that on a planet warmed by our greenhouse gases they'll become more frequent still in the next. And Galapagos penguins, already the rarest of penguins, perhaps absent.

In public talks around the globe the scientist shows pictures of the black-and-white-suited birds hunched on their volcanic island, peering out to sea. "Sentinels," she calls them, signaling us that we've greatly disrupted the winds and oceans, warning us and our lives by losing theirs.

Staghorn Coral

He remembers the first time he tipped off a boat into the waters of Key Largo. Gliding through the body of blue silence, he gradually began to hear it crackle and buzz—the mouths of hundreds of fish, feeding. A living kaleidoscope of them swirled around what looked like deer antlers anchored to the bottom. The antlers stretched for acres, vast stands spread like a forest in the sea.

These, he learned, were not rocks or bones or stone-hard plants, but animals, soft-bodied ones. Thousands of the creatures, called polyps, composed every set of antlers. A single, pinhead-size polyp had cloned itself, sucking calcium from the water to make a protective limestone cup for each new, clear-jellied polyp-body. Budding, branching its rack as large as a car, the polyp community not only profited itself; it also offered food and shelter for creatures swimming by. Everywhere he dove in the Keys that summer of 1978, he saw staghorn colonies covering the ocean floor. Other more colorful corals he enjoyed, but this builder, protector, and provider he admired.

Forty years later, he's finally in the right place at the right time to see the reef builders' virtuoso display. He's seen staghorns' workaday craft. If a storm or a shark breaks off a branch, its polyp inhabitants simply lay down new limestone foundations wherever they fall. But tonight, these stoic toilers will dazzle. It's the fourth night after August's full moon, the one night every polyp in every staghorn colony along 350 miles of the Florida Reef Tract launches a blizzard of tiny translucent globes.

At the surface the globes break apart, spilling the eggs and sperm of each colony onto the waves to find mates from a different colony. The lucky ones become larvae, baby corals swimming, searching for the light, temperature, pH, and sound of a hospitable bottom-home. Place matters. Each miniscule larva aims to establish a colony lasting centuries.

As the summer night deepens, he waits in a boat with a half dozen others. Earlier in the evening they had dived down thirty feet and draped tent-nets over what looked like old-fashioned TV antennae made of PVC pipe and anchored to the bottom. From the branches of these "trees" pieces of staghorn coral hung like ornaments. At 10 PM the team leader signals them overboard again. Swimming to a tree he had tented earlier, he watches a bottle at the net's tip fill with tiny globes. In each globe throb dozens of aspiring staghorns.

The sheer profusion of the spawn—of the coral's will to continue—makes what he'd seen a few days before starker still. He'd been told, he'd seen pictures. He thought he understood. But when he swam the reef, re-creating the route of his teenage dive-adventure, he felt the statistic—97 percent—hit like a grounded ship in his gut. From Key Largo to the Dry Tortugas, where he remembered miles of ochre antlers crackling with brilliant fish, he now saw mounds of gray rubble. All of them vacant and silent, some stinking of newly dead polyp-flesh.

The devastation began in 1979. White-band disease began to sweep the reef, sped by warming waters. Fastest growing of corals, the staghorns had barely begun to recover when, in 1982, a temperature spike—El Niño driven—flash-fried most of the remaining colonies. It happened again in 1998 and in 2016. Ninety-seven percent of staghorn coral colonies lay rotting on the ocean floor.

When he touched the gray rubble, the limestone skeletons of the once-pulsing reef builders crumbled in his hands. Heat-bleached, the polyps had starved. Though they provide feeding stations for multitudes, staghorn corals cannot feed themselves. So they invite into their cells zooxanthellae, an algae that uses its power of photosynthesis to make food for the corals—and, as a bonus, colors their clear-bodied hosts the yellow-brown-green shades of algae bodies. In return for food and beauty, the corals hide zooxanthellae from the many algae-eating mouths of the sea.

Their collaboration works exquisitely in the water temperatures that have bathed the Keys for six thousand years. But when the water heats above the highest temperatures these sea creatures have known and stays there week after week, the algae's photosynthesis short-circuits, leaking by-products toxic to coral. Shocked, the polyps evict their colorful and necessary guests. Left empty and hungry, the corals die unless the water soon cools.

Capping the collection bottle, he swims it to the boat. Had the coral globes spilled wild from their home colonies into the sea, the eggs and sperm inside would have died unfertilized. They will couple only with those not their colony-kin, and the staghorn colonies still alive in the Keys are too few and too far between for their gametes to meet.

The boat speeds to a lab on shore where others wait. They open all the bottles, separate eggs from sperm, and introduce them to unrelated mates in different bottles. As they wait, genetically new staghorn embryos come to life. Then, gently, they tuck the tiny coral infants into carefully regulated nursery tanks and start a 'round-the-clock vigil. He asks for the night watch.

Gazing into the water at creatures he cannot see, he imagines their future: growing in the lab to fingertip-size, then hung on PVC trees in the sea, harvested at cantaloupe-size, and planted on the very reef where their ancestors died. Where they too might die in waters human life heats too hot for coral life. He knows the dire prognosis. Still, he volunteers to be a coral midwife and reef planter. Beneath his fear and despair he is still the young admirer of small soft-bodied animals bound together, building shelter for the ocean's multitudes.

The Sick

Panamanian Golden Frog

Crouched on a streamside boulder, a bright yellow frog no longer than a child's thumb lifts his head, and whistles. Another male has invaded his territory and must be warned. But the percussive ruckus of the stream somersaulting down-mountain mutes all other musics. To make his message indisputably clear, the defender puts himself squarely in eyeshot of the trespasser—and waves. Not an upward punch, nor a manic flapping, but a slow rotation, widespread hand lifting chest high, circling deliberately out-to-side, in, and slowly down on his rock.

"Semaphoring," this waving is called, the golden frog's novel and ingenious adaptation to his noisy home. Along the mountain streams of central Panama, water-rush deafened his ancestors. Eardrums, assaulted, vanished from their anatomy. This day's male still hears some frequencies—through his skin, it seems. But when life's urgencies demand more than his impaired hearing and puny voice can muster, he relies on the mode of communication his fore-frogs evolved over epochs in splashy cacophony: sign language.

The interloper sees the slow-circling wave. And waves back, twice. The two have understood each other perfectly. The defender has no choice. He leaps the distance between them and onto the other's back and with one hand forces his competitor's head down till his soft throat scrapes rock. Overcome, the prone frog remains prone, submissive. The stronger swaggers back to his boulder-post and refocuses his attention on the desire that set him there, watching.

When she appears he has a wave for her too. And she for him. She allows him to climb aboard her much larger back and clasp her tightly mid-torso. Bonded at stream's edge, they may stay embraced for two days or two weeks or two months. In her own time, she'll release a long, looped strand of almost four hundred seed pearl-size eggs, and he, simultaneously, the sperm to fertilize them. She has chosen the site carefully. When she lets the sticky strand go over that gritty rock in the shallows, it will catch and hold fast.

Brown-black and flecked in gold, the fishlike tadpoles that hatch metamorphose into leggy green froglets hidden on mossy green rocks. Eating an insect smorgasbord, the froglets turn traffic-light yellow, their backs usually splotched in black. Eye-catching, not eye-avoiding, is their new strategy. Bite-size, they wave to catch predators' attention, shining their yellow warning: *Eat me and writhe.* Glands between their shoulder blades secrete a nerve poison toxic enough to kill a thousand mice.

But rather than deter, their brilliance attracted one predator. Wearing gloves against the toxin, collectors once tramped through Panama's forests, snatching up bags of gold in plain view. Ever since pre-Columbian peoples carved their images on petroglyphs, Panamanian golden frogs have symbolized good fortune. Locals kept them as talismans, hoteliers put them in lobbies and sold them to tourists, collectors traded them around the globe. More and more people wanted more and more luck.

And more people wanted to live and do business in the beauty of the frogs' lush mountain home. Bulldozers and tractors cleared forests; trash, pesticides, and fertilizers fouled streams. But even the loss of their home was not the golden frogs' worst stroke of luck.

Maybe it came in the bag of a collector or on the boots of a road builder. No one knows exactly how or when. But in 2004, biologists began finding Panama's national animal belly up in and alongside streams. A microscopic predator had slipped over the border from Costa Rica where it had already decimated that country's frogs. Within six months it destroyed half of all frog species in a protected region of western Panama, including the area's golden frogs. And it was moving east.

Stealthy, spore borne, the fungus with an eleven-syllable name—called "chytrid" for short—attacks frogs' most vulnerable organ. Unlike other animals, most amphibians drink and breathe through their skin. Chytrid thickens frogs' skin so water and electrolytes can't get in. Reflexes go slack; skin peels back. Finally, the three-chambered heart convulses and stops. An amphibian black plague, chytrid has erased ninety species in the past three decades, and it threatens to do the same to four hundred more. Researchers have called it "the most destructive pathogen ever described by science." The genus to which golden frogs belong has suffered most.

In early 2006, a Panamanian biologist guarding the last three streams with living golden frogs began finding them slowed, skin-ravaged, and dead. To his alert, scores of volunteers responded, scooping up the last wild goldens before chytrid took them. The biologist and his wife began caring for them and other chytrid-threatened species in disinfected glass boxes stacked in a building at a nearby zoo. A better refuge has since been built; still they call it an "amphibian ark."

Inside the ark, it's not a matter of waiting for the wave of plague to pass. Loose in the world now, chytrid can't be contained. It will always be lapping at the door. Every day scientists in labs around the world search for ways to make amphibians chytrid resistant. They dream of releasing golden frogs from their glass boxes into raucous mountain streams, and they plead with citizens to protect those streams. Meanwhile a hundred thousand people each year come to the ark to peer at the few lucky-unlucky kept behind glass. Sometimes the frogs wave. The visitors want to see *hello*, not *goodbye*. But nobody can really say.

Indiana Bat

Through thick layers of absolute sleep she feels heat rising in the body pressed tightly against her left side. Her right side too warms with the warming of the body pressed there. Pressed against her chest, another body seeps heat to hers just as the one behind her warms. Soon these bodies—and hundreds more—are rustling. Hers, with the help of her neighbors', heats, and her heart, with theirs, quickens—forty, ninety, two hundred, six hundred beats each minute. In just an hour every cell in her has surged from nearly dead to urgently alive. She snaps open her wings and falls into the swirl of tiny furred bodies flapping through the cave.

It is a communal resurrection. And in a healthy colony of Indiana bats it happens every thirteen days or so for the six months of their hibernation. Near-death sleep mightily strains the body. When circulation slows to a trickle, toxins collect, tissues begin to sicken. At the brink of harm, an internal alarm rouses each and all. They wake and fly, flushing the toxins from their systems. After about an hour of freshening, they regather, toes grabbing the cave's nubbled ceiling. They fold their wings and scooch together, four hundred upside-down bodies squeezed into each square foot. As one body, they close their eyes and surrender again to the slowing that will save them until the world outside warms.

They slow so dangerously near death because they trust the group-body. And because they trust this cave. It is a rare place, as they have known for thousands of years. Long, high, many-entranced, the cave's architecture keeps its temperature between thirty-seven and forty-five degrees Fahrenheit. Other bats can live well in warmer or colder caves, but not this most sensitive and companionable of all North American species. The weight of three pennies in a palm, each Indiana bat arrives with just enough body fat to survive six months of communal hibernation. If the air were warmer, their group sleep would not be as deep, its faster metabolism using up body fat. If the air were cooler or drier, they would sleep more deeply but wake more often to flush toxins, using up body fat. This cave holds them perfectly poised in a sleep neither too shallow nor too deep, so their fat stores will last until spring supplies insects to eat.

Humans too flock to these exceptional caves—for exploration, intrigue, and income. When flushed from their winter refuges, bat colonies freeze or starve. Ten million Indiana bats once sheltered in Kentucky's Mammoth Cave; now four hundred thousand sightseers tour it every year. In 1967, there were so few of the species that it was one of the first listed in the Endangered Species Protection Act. Four decades of protection later, the U.S. Fish and Wildlife Service declared the Indiana bat had a "high recovery potential."

Then in February 2006, in a cave adjoining tourist caverns near Albany, New York, a spelunker photographed hibernating bats whose noses were oddly chalked with a white powder. The following winter state biologists found several hundred bats dead in four caves nearby, their noses powdered white. Within ten years, seven million bats of nine species had died in thirty-one states. Biologists named the plague "white-nose syndrome."

The very places Indiana bats trusted to preserve them betrayed them. Cool, dark, and humid, cave air not only holds bats in metabolic equipoise, it also invigorates a fungus new to North America. Brought from Europe on spelunkers' gear, spores of the fungus multiplied rampantly in caves of northeastern states, then spread farther and faster on the bodies of bats. The tightly packed group-body that Indiana bats trusted to heat them and hold them through winter contaminated them.

When spores of the fungus stick to her body, a hibernating bat becomes a furred petri dish. The fungus grows most densely on her nose. But it invades at her most vulnerable portal. Eighty-five percent of her body's surface, a bat's wings are exquisitely laced with blood and lymph vessels, nerves, glands, muscle, and connective tissue. All the rhythms of her body pulse within their thin skin membranes. The fungus simply devours every sort of cell in them. The winged jazz she is collapses into a jumble.

The biologist who has been watching this cave for two winters finds her outside in the middle of a February day. She is wing-walking feebly across the snow. She stops and licks up a few flakes. He takes her in his palm, touches her tiny white nose. Her wing membrane looks like crumpled tissue paper. It sticks to his finger. Emaciated and dazed, she doesn't resist when he puts her in a box to take back to his lab, where he knows she will die within hours. Inside the cave he finds others of her colony flying crazily near the entrance. Eating their wings, the fungus is short-circuiting their metabolism, jolting them awake, thirsty, driving them to fly a crippled flight, using up body fat. He will soon be scooping them into his box too.

All the autopsies on the two-inch bodies tell the same story. While scientists research treatments of several kinds, they believe the best hope rests within the bats themselves. Their European cousins, over time, developed immunity to white-nose syndrome. Biologists are seeing signs of another sort of life-restoring force in Indiana bats. Some remnant populations, rather than waking once every thirteen nights of their hibernation, are rousing each night—briefly, without burning much fat. Warming together more often, the colony keeps the cold-loving plague at bay. Though it seemed to destroy them, the bats have found deep within the group-body a force that answers death with resurrection.

Koala

The woman stands outside her back door and scans the trees at the edge of her lot. She has done this every morning since she moved to this suburb. It was November. Around midnight she jolted awake to screams, bellows, and barking dogs. Next morning, filling the birdbath, she saw her: a soft gray bundle propped in the fork of a eucalyptus tree, sunlight on her white ear tufts making mini-haloes on either side of her head.

All day and into the evening the koala stayed there, shifting now and then, or splaying over a branch. She spent each day this way, a marvel of adaptation to the available. The leaves of her eucalyptus tree are not only tough; they're toxic to most other animals. Capitalizing on the lack of competition, koalas long ago became eucalypt specialists, their anatomy adapting to a food others avoided. They evolved a caecum—a section of the gut tract—proportionally larger than any other mammal's. There, masticated leaf paste stews, millions of bacteria eking from it every possible atom of nutrition. It's so much inner work for so little return that koalas must rest about twenty hours a day, directing what energy their diet does yield back into digestion.

And the various rituals of mating. In November, spring is full-blown in eastern Australia, and male koalas are straining their scanty energy reserves, moving through their home ranges, marking trees, chasing females, and bellowing at any rival with a ferocity shocking for a creature of such amiable appearance. Often, on her evening commute, the woman saw one waddle-trotting across the road, or dead beside it.

After the raucous November nights, she suspected the female asleep in her tree was not alone. Though true, she had no visible proof. The joey born just thirty-five days after his mother mated had the size and semblance of a pink jellybean. Hairless, blind, earless, still he managed to climb from the birth canal through his mother's fur and into her pouch, sniffing his route to the two teats inside. Once in his miniscule mouth, the teat swelled, latching him fast to his life-milk. His mother tightened her pouch sphincter, setting a double lock on his nursery.

Five months later, fully furred and bright eyed, the joey was still tucked into the pouch. If the woman had stood below his mother's resting tree, if she had looked up through binoculars at just the right moment, she could have seen him peep out and lean down to eat a greenish ooze from her rectum. Called "pap," it's full of her gut microflora; he must have it in his gut to digest eucalyptus leaves.

By July the woman needed no binoculars. A miniature of his mother, the koala babe surveyed the yard from her back. Thanks to the pap, he was eating eucalyptus now, though he also pushed his head into her pouch to nurse. Both koalas smelled pleasantly of cough drops. They murmured to each other, mother and child. To the woman sitting in a chair, listening, it sounded like prayer.

Because the koalas moved among the trees in her yard and the adjoining park, she didn't see them for days at a time. Early one evening she saw the joey on a branch, looking down. On the ground his mother squatted as if to urinate, and cried. Alerted, the dog in the next yard barked and lunged, the woman ran between it and the koala, who heaved herself at the tree, and as she climbed, laboriously, the woman saw her wet, brown-stained backside. The joey rushed to his mother and clung as she pulled herself onto the lowest branch and slumped.

From TV news stories the woman knew the signs of late-stage koala chlamydia. Nearly all koalas carry the disease, brought to Australia in the bodies of colonists' sheep. But in the bodies of koalas at ease in a land of abundant eucalyptus trees, the bacteria lay dormant. Koalas thrived. Ten million slept in the trees a century ago, before hunters shot several million for their luxurious fur. Public outcry at the slaughter compelled the government to protect koala bodies. But not koala homelands. Because where koalas must live—the country's eucalyptus-rich southeast coast—humans want to live.

When bulldozers ripped out her home and food trees for subdivisions and roads and shops, the mother koala ran to the park behind the woman's yard. As did other refugees. Crowded, hungry, they often fight. Cars and dogs kill many. Survivors live in perpetual stress. And in koala bodies under stress, long-latent chlamydia wakes and flares.

Volunteers from the koala hospital came when the woman called. She followed their van and stayed while the hospital director pulled away the squealing joey, then sedated and examined his mother: urinary and genital tracts inflamed. Too infected for antibiotics to help. She would be euthanized. The joey? Yes, chlamydia positive, passed in his mother's milk, but in an early stage. In him, antibiotics should clear it. When grown, he'll be released to his home range, the park behind the woman's house. Where he'll get chlamydia from stressed mates.

The woman moaned.

A lot of us feel that way, the director said. From a crate, she picked up the motherless joey. He clung to her. *His story is our story now, isn't it?*

Driving home the woman sees a bulldozer mowing over trees in the way of a new shopping mall. Back in her yard she sits where she had often listened to the mother and child murmuring to each other. In the silence, her pent-up tears come. Somehow, she knows, she must tell their story.

Black-footed Ferret

On a mound of dirt on a wind-combed prairie in northern Wyoming, the rarest mammal in North America is dancing. He prances and bucks, then stops. Then hops—forward, forward, backward, side-hop left—spins around, and dives into the hole at the center of the mound. A four-beat wait. His black bandit mask peeks over the rim. Then he flings the muscular tube of his torso out again into the prairie dawn, bounding, twisting, frisking for an audience of none.

He is fully grown, an adult, not a play-inclined kit. His jaunty moves are not meant to confuse predator or prey, attract a mate, or warn companions. The only reason for his dance is ferret-ness. Curious and quick, lithe and strong, black-footed ferrets often dance just because they are, just because they can.

Audaciously alive, this ferret ends his dance as the sun rises and slips underground to sleep away the day in a burrow that a prairie dog clan abandoned. His short fur and slender shape insulate him poorly against prairie cold; he needs the reliable warmth of their underground home. It's his hermitage now, a base from which he'll range a mile or more in the dark of the March night, looking for the emerald eyeshine of a female willing to mate in the nearest empty prairie dog den. Because he ate last night—catching a prairie dog asleep, killing it cleanly with a bite to the windpipe—he has food cached away for two more days. Besides food, prairie dogs supply another essential for a ferret on the hunt. Should a badger, coyote, or bobcat target his emerald eyeshine and pounce, prairie dog holes provide his surest escape hatch.

For nearly a million years, prairie dogs and ferrets lived together well in the heart of North America. Prairie dogs fed ferrets and sheltered them. Ferrets culled prairie dog colonies to a size the land could support. Both communities thrived. At one time a million black-footed ferrets lived among hundreds of millions of prairie dogs on grasslands that stretched between Saskatchewan and Mexico.

Within 150 years the prairie dog towns were plowed up or poisoned. To the pioneers planting crops and grazing livestock to feed the growing hunger of a growing nation, prairie dogs were competitors for the rich land. By 1980, a mere 2 percent were left, holding on in small colonies cut off from one another. As prairie dogs go, so go ferrets—faster. By 1980, nobody had seen one of the wild dancers for six years. Biologists considered them extinct in the wild.

The following year a Wyoming ranch dog named Shep brought a dead black-footed ferret to his owners' door. Biologists converged on the ranch, sweeping flashlights across its thousands of acres by night, searching for emerald eyeshine. They found 129 of the extinct species alive and multiplying among the prairie dogs of two neighboring ranches.

Then in 1985, distemper and sylvatic plague—a flea-borne disease brought to North America from Asia—infested the ranches' prairie dog towns. A plague-infected prairie dog is certain to die. The biologists watching knew that as prairie dogs go, so go ferrets—faster. For two years, they spent their nights trapping the ferrets that had not yet fallen to the plague ravaging their prairie dog hosts. On a cold night in February 1987, they caught the last wild black-footed ferret, a large male they named "Scarface," and took him away in a pickup truck.

The risk these biologists had taken excited them and terrified them. Had they rescued the world's eighteen remaining black-footed ferrets from certain death in the wild only to watch them die in cages? No one had successfully bred the creatures in captivity. They worked slowly, methodically, consulting every known expert. They hoped. Some prayed.

In the spring of 1987, Scarface fathered two litters of kits. Since then, nine thousand black-footed ferrets have been born in carefully controlled captivity, and most of those have been released into prairie dog towns at sites across the West—including the ranch that was home to Scarface. It is his descendant now dancing there at dawn.

He doesn't know his survival chances are slim. He is still the rarest mammal in North America, and is apt to be, until prairie dogs receive some measure of the devotion that has saved him. Researchers, understanding the symbiosis of the two species, have developed a peanut-butter-flavored vaccine that prairie dogs love and that makes them immune to sylvatic plague. That means ferrets too are spared—if nearly all the prairie dogs at a ferret-release site eat a vaccine. How to be sure every prairie dog takes his peanut-butter-flavored medicine is biologists' next feat.

But all the efforts to protect prairie dogs in order to protect ferrets will work only if farmers and ranchers choose to see the dogs differently. The owners of this ranch have. When they described how a cattle operation works, conservationists listened and eased restrictions on what they could and could not do on their land. Ranchers listened when conservationists described prairie dogs as not only hosts extraordinaire for ferrets, but also the anchors of an intricately ordered homeplace for more than one hundred species found nowhere else on Earth. At the end of the conversation, the ranchers asked to have black-footed ferrets brought home to the land from which their eighteen ancestors were taken. Pledging to protect the ferrets, they've pledged to respect the prairie dogs. They are, they see, a new kind of pioneer.

WEEK THREE

The Homeless

Monarch Butterfly
(Eastern North America population)

Gazing at the canopy sweeping up a hundred feet, the young man turns his face to receive a ray of sun. As his skin warms he waits for the moment to arrive. He hears it before he sees it—a susurration, like gentle rain. What seem to be clumps of dead leaves bowing the branches are breaking apart and bursting orange into the air, like sparks from the long-dead volcano this mountain is. Warmed enough for flight, thousands of little flames rise and glide on wings softly beating a rain song—fire and rain on a bright November afternoon.

The monarchs are roosting again in their winter palaces. The young man used to hike here with his father, who cut the trees with a logging crew. That was before they knew that the butterflies come only here, millions of them, from the Great Plains to the Atlantic Ocean, streaming south down a flyway that funnels them into Texas, then up, all the millions, to twelve cloud-forest pockets in central Mexico to rest in the fir trees.

The monarchs have no memory of this place. They were born in the north. But when the days grew shorter and the nights colder, they turned south, consulting the compass of the sun. Somewhere in Mexico, charged particles in their wings and bodies crackled. Metals in the volcanic rocks of this mountain range drew them like paperclips to a magnet. In waves they descended to trees called the "sacred firs," a kingdom they had never seen. One lights on the man's open hand. She weighs less than a paperclip and has flown, perhaps, three thousand miles from Canada. From all over the world people come to gaze at these wafer-thin, radiant pilgrims.

The logger's son guides the gazers every winter day to the butterflies' refuge. Last summer, when the monarchs emerged as adults in the north, their reproductive systems were stunted, all energies conscripted for the great migration south and for winter survival in Mexico. But come March, an internal signal shudders each one; their reproductive organs surge. The monarchs scatter from the fir boughs in a flurry of mating. And then lift north.

Within three days some have flown as far as Texas. From the air females intently smell the landscape. Receptors on their legs and antennae can smell a single, inch-tall milkweed sunk in a sea of vegetation. They are avid for milkweed. It is the only plant on which they will lay their pinhead-size eggs. For about a month each female plants four hundred or so eggs, one at a time, along a northerly row. Then she, and all the monarchs born the summer before, who flew together to Mexico and partway back, fold their wings and die.

Ninety-nine in a hundred of their eggs perish. But on the third day, from the one remaining, a caterpillar the size of a rice grain breaks. She devours the egg casing, then the milkweed leaves beneath her feet. In those leaves is a steroid that makes her body brightly striped—and toxic to her predators. Ravenous, she eats milkweed unceasingly for twelve days, bulging her skin to splitting. Five skins later, two thousand times her birthweight, she stops. She knows her moment. Crawling to a suitable twig or ledge, she hangs head down, shaping herself into a question mark.

One last time her skin falls away. This new one is not a soft, stripy, caterpillar skin but a polished, jade-green shell studded with a gold tiara. Because she is enclosed and still, changes that had already begun within her wormlike body erupt outward. Wings! Long, delicate legs! After twelve days in the chrysalis she is a new creature—and cramped. She pushes out into the wide air and pumps her wings dry, quivering for flight.

Like her mother, she too will fly north, laying eggs, sipping wildflowers. Unlike her mother, she will live just one month, not eight. Her offspring will replay her month-long life, arriving by May in the Midwest, searching for milkweed in seas of corn and soybeans. By some logic scientists don't yet understand, monarchs prefer milkweed growing among agricultural crops, laying four times as many eggs there as on milkweed elsewhere.

If they can find it. In twenty years, 99 percent of the milkweed here has disappeared. In those twenty years, farmers have been spraying their fields with glyphosate, marketed as "Roundup." The corn and soybeans have been genetically modified to withstand the herbicide, so farmers spray often, all through the growing season. The food crops live on, but milkweed is killed at the root. Up and down and across the crop rows female monarchs flutter, searching for the home their offspring must have. Some, straying, find a few milkweed stems along unmown roadsides. Just a few. A billion monarchs used to soar to Mexico, most of them reared on Midwestern milkweed. Since the introduction of Roundup, 90 percent of the bright pilgrims have vanished.

The news has not escaped farmers. In coffee shops they talk about government programs that will pay them for letting tilled land go fallow, or even for planting land in milkweed, native grasses, and flowers. All of them hold considerable debt for land and equipment; they lose sleep over roller-coaster commodity prices, trade wars, and erratic weather. Investing in butterflies is another card in a risky hand.

But when their children come home with milkweed shoots from the butterfly gardens they've planted at school and tell them about the amazing super-monarchs that fly all the way to Mexico, that are dying and might soon be gone forever, when they ask, *Where can we plant this milkweed?* some of the farmers decide to take a royal gamble.

North Atlantic Right Whale

S he's called "Kleenex," though the researchers looking for her don't know why. When first sighted in 1977, she was a young mother, guiding her first calf into the Bay of Fundy's summer pastures. In the decades since, she's nursed seven more calves in birthing waters off Georgia and Florida, lolling on her back, baby balanced on her belly in the sun. With twenty-two children, grandchildren, and great-grandchildren, she's a grand matriarch in the world's smallest population of great whales.

But she hasn't mothered a calf since 2009. Researchers in the surveillance plane scanning the sea north of Cape Cod's toe on April 10, 2018, wanted badly to see Kleenex. And they were afraid to see Kleenex.

It may seem easy to spot a creature the length of a school bus weighing 150,000 pounds and periodically sighing a V-shaped spume of mist fifteen feet into the air. Especially since right whales, more blubberous and thus more buoyant than any other cetacean species, spend more time at the surface. And lying still at the surface, like massive black logs. And often near shore. In fact, they were so near and numerous in the 1600s that the Pilgrims claimed they could walk across Cape Cod Bay on the backs of right whales. One account tallied twenty-nine harpooned in the bay on a single day in 1700. Conveniently, its two-foot-thick blubber undercoat made each corpse easy to float to shore for butchering; boiled, the blubber yielded 1,300 gallons of lucrative oil. To whalers, these were, indeed, the "right whales" to hunt.

Though they are still massive and slow, frequenters of surface and shore, they are not easy to spot. There are too few of them—maybe four hundred. Fewer than one hundred are breeding females, and these are dying faster than males. It's an equation trending toward extinction. Those who keep watch believe the species cannot afford to lose the fecund Kleenex.

Staring from the plane on that April day, they searched for a break in the hypnotic chop and roll of the waves—a bus-size shadow crowned with a white splotch that looks nothing like a Kleenex. Researchers recognize right whales by their splotches. "Callosities" they're called—raised patches of rough skin on the chin, upper lip, brow, and crown. Pale lice colonize these patches, helpfully eating dying skin and creating white-on-black shapes unique to each whale. Fiddle, Armada, Anchor, Starry Night: these whales wear their names plain as a tattoo. The researcher who named Kleenex— one of the first to be named—didn't record a reason.

After hours in the air someone called out, *There!* The pilot banked and a crew member called the hotline in Provincetown: *Right whale 1142, Kleenex, off Stellwagen Bank, still entangled.*

When they last sighted her in 2014, the survey team saw a thick braided rope wrapped around Kleenex's upper jaw and the top of her head. Then she vanished. Each year since, they've feared that one of the right whales found dead on a beach or floating at sea will be she. Of 2017's seventeen corpses, one was her granddaughter Couplet.

Before the rope bound it, Kleenex could open her mouth wide enough to admit a swimming pool's worth of water. She could freely press her soft tongue, the size of a small car, against the roof of her mouth, streaming the water out through five hundred baleen hanging from her upper jaw. Like eight-foot-long Venetian blinds fringed with bristles, the baleen trap bushels of creatures the size of rice grains. Kleenex needs to eat a ton of these tiny animals every day. After nearly four years wrapped in heavy rope, the mountain of blubber at the base of her skull has sunk into a wrinkled ravine. Her once-glossy black skin has dulled. She is slowly starving.

Once before, Kleenex had been entangled; then, rope wrapped the base of her tail. She flailed it off, but not before it left bright white scars—the other markings by which researchers identify 85 percent of surviving right whales. Ropes hang throughout their home range. Connected to lobster and crab traps on the sea bottom, the lines rise to buoys that show fishermen where to find their catch. Each year the ropes catch about fifty right whales. For most, like Kleenex, it will not be the first time. Even when not wrapped around their mouths, a rope's drag and the wounds it opens drain these leviathans by ounces. Females, already straining their energy reserves trying to bear calves, die sooner.

Keeping Kleenex in view, the aerial team directed a rescue boat to her. The boat crew's usual MO—attaching buoys to the entangling rope to keep a whale from diving while they cut her free—was futile here. Kleenex's shackle trailed no line for attaching a buoy. Bracing himself, the crew leader raised a crossbow.

For two cold, windy days they followed her, unable to get a clean shot. On the third day she surfaced fifty feet away, head tilted to see them. Taking aim, the bowman froze, caught in her dark, liquid eye. Someone yelled, and he fired an arrow tipped with four razor-sharp blades at her head. The crew saw the blades split some of the rope strands before the great whale fled.

Survey teams look for her still. They hope that in time the frayed ropes will fall away—in time to save her and the calves she could yet bear. Her species needs every calf until researchers and fishermen design workable, affordable crab and lobster traps without the lines that mangle whales. Fishermen don't want to catch whales. They, too, have been caught in that dark, deep-knowing eye.

Polar Bear

The gusty Arctic wind finger-combs her coat down to the skin. Autumn has finally come to the southern Beaufort Sea, and it finds her restless. Through whorls of snow she studies the waves chopping at the ice floe's edge.

In spring, when seal hunting was better, she and other members of this sea's polar bear clan mated. Five years old, it was her first time. Immediately her body began urging her to eat—and eat more. It insisted she add at least 220 pounds to her 500 before allowing the fertilized egg to implant in her womb. She lay at holes in the ice shelf near shore waiting for seals to pop up for air or haul out to molt. As the days warmed and the ice retreated farther from shore and seals, she followed it, eating less and less until—unlikely luck!—she found the carcass of a young beluga whale caught in a breathing hole. Thanks to his body, hers will give birth.

Now, in late October, she rides the ice inching toward shore again. She must den soon and would like to do it on ice over shallow waters. Then, when she wakes in spring, her first seal-meal will be near her door. Her mother made her first den on near-shore ice thirty years ago. But now near-shore waters stay ice-free weeks longer, and pack ice stable enough for a den lies miles behind her. Shall she turn around and trek there, burning precious fat stores she's packed away for cubs-to-come? She chooses to leap.

The scientists who radio-collared her after she mated know she's swimming. They hold their breath. Between the edge of the pack ice and land, two hundred miles of open water chop and roll. Her front paws, big as dinner plates, paddle hard while her back limbs rudder. She swims through the night, and the next day, and night. Stumbling ashore, she sprawls on the frozen sand and sleeps. The scientists exhale.

Never has she—nor her mother nor her grandmother—left the sea ice. Waking on a barrier island off Alaska's North Slope, she walks inland considering snowdrifts. Finding one of satisfactory height and density, she digs a cave just large enough to turn around in. From inside she punches a hole in the roof for air. Then she curls up while windblown snow seals the door.

About Christmastime two cubs the size of guinea pigs tumble from her, helpless and hungry. Nursing, they drain two pounds from her every day. She thins, they enlarge. By March the den has become too snug for comfort, and she, ravenous.

On a video monitor the scientists see the den's airhole explode as her head and shoulders burst through. As she stands, stunned by sunlight, they note her slack flanks. When she lets the cubs follow her through the opened roof, she has to turn and tug one out.

Around the den the twin males learn to tumble and run. One always loses their races. He is appreciably smaller than his twenty-five-pound twin. His mother's long swim last autumn burned fat stores that would have made enough milk for two hungry mouths.

To save him and herself she knows she must eat seal, soon. Blubbery ringed seals are the one food both energy-rich enough and attainable for her. But they are becoming less attainable as greenhouse gases warm the planet. No polar bear can outswim a seal. To hunt them she needs an ice platform, and each year more of that floor dissolves beneath her.

After twelve days, she knows she must leave land before winter's near-shore ice breaks up. Chuffing at the cubs to follow, she walks onto the frozen sea. Her keen nose detects the breath of a seal exhaling at a hole half a mile away. She hurries the cubs there and camps, waiting for the creature that will save them.

She has three months over seal-abundant waters to restore herself for her cubs, still nursing voraciously. But because, in the den, her body used up all its fat stores, then began burning muscle, she's now a weak, clumsy hunter. Instead of the seal every five days her body craves, she's catching one a week, when she's lucky.

In September, the scientists find her on the barrier island again, scavenging with other hungry bears at a pile of whale bones Inupiat hunters left for them. The senior researcher pictures what happened. As the summer sun melted near-shore ice, she retreated with the ice to deeper, seal-sparse waters—till hunger pitched her forward. She shimmied on thin ice, keeping her cubs out of water as long as possible and then, when it wasn't, urging them onto floe after floe, until there were none.

As she rips scraps of meat from the towering bones, he's relieved to see the larger cub tucked beneath her. But he imagines the little one—bleating, floundering in the waves—and her—moaning, frantic, tiring, finally turning away, heaving toward shore. It's a story he knows too well. Over three decades he's seen the number of bears in the southern Beaufort Sea cut nearly in half. Populations in other seas that are stable now will be living this clan's story if greenhouse gases are not curbed.

New research questions intrigue him, but he's left active science. Because the linchpin question has been answered: no Arctic ice, no polar bears. He works now to tell this story with every tool and technology, especially to children. Webcasting from the tundra, he shows them the magnificent white bears outside his door. One young boy asks, *Will we lose them, all the polar bears?*

I don't know, the man answers. *Maybe. We don't have to. Will you help me?*

Lowland Tapir

Asleep in the heat of late afternoon, he wakes when his body senses the tree shadows stretching. Even before heaving his bulk up off the forest floor he too is stretching—reaching, circling his snout and upper lip, grown together into a stubby trunk, to read the day's news and weather. No warnings in the air, so he chooses his usual, well-worn route to the marsh. Along the way his dexterous nose grabs leaves from saplings or snuffles the ground for pequi fruits fallen since yesterday's walkalong. Eating, though, is not his desire-of-the-moment.

Coming to the pond, his toes—four in front, three in back, each one a neat little hoof—splay for traction on the muddy bank. He steps in steady as a five-hundred-pound prince and walks deeper, deeper, till even the tips of his ears disappear. Lifting his snout above the surface like a snorkel, he feels the water wash him clean of the day's dust and biting bugs. For a few minutes, underwater, he drifts off to sleep.

Had he been born here forty years before, his pond entry might have been a running dive, escape from a jaguar keen for tapir meat. The water would have bathed old claw scars on the thick crest beneath his mane. This tapir has never met a jaguar. And water no longer saves him.

When dusk drenches the air purple, South America's largest and oldest mammal, survivor of twenty million years of change, strokes across the pond and nimbly climbs the opposite bank. Now he is intent on eating. His barrel-body pushes through a narrow belt of forest and pokes out onto a gaping expanse. He waves his snout, sniffing for cows. Alone tonight, he trots across the planted grasses but slows when he does smell cows, their odor stuffed inside an acrid cloud. Suddenly the ground shakes and a mad roar hurtles toward him and past in a whirlwind. Trembling, he waits until he hears nothing, nothing but insects. Then he runs, hooves beating a frantic rhythm across the rock-hard strip splitting the pasture.

In the morning, when the scientist downloads location data from his GPS collar, she can't see what a close call this tapir had with a cattle truck, only that he crossed one of the busiest highways in Brazil's Cerrado. She traces his route through more pasture to a soybean field where he spent the night, grazing.

When she and her team veterinarian knelt beside him, anesthetized in the capture pen a year ago, he seemed robust and fine, a prime young male about five years old. They took measurements, blood and skin samples. Then gently they curled back the fleshy snout to look inside his mouth: teeth broken, teeth missing, swollen gums. Grimacing, the two women snapped pictures and fit the collar to his thick neck. *We'll call this one Tomás*, the scientist said. She stroked the tapir's ears, half moons edged in white. She found them, crowning his bulk, a delightfully delicate touch.

Now when she examines tapirs in the Cerrado she expects ravaged mouths. Her team's hypotheses revolve around food. Brazilians long ago named their savannah, richer in native plants and animals than any savannah on the planet, Cerrado—meaning "closed," meaning worthless for agriculture. Then in the 1960s, as human hunger for beef sharpened, American agronomists discovered that pouring lime on Cerrado soil made it yield bumper crops of the corn and soybeans fed to cattle and other farmed animals. Native grasses could be plowed under and replaced with alien grasses that fed much larger herds. The "worthless" Cerrado—now being cleared faster than the Amazon—has been made a booming agribusiness. Losing their homes, the few tapirs left have lost the food their teeth evolved to eat. The food they find is coated with pesticides. On their wrecked enamel the scientist reads the story of a food chain broken at every link.

Scrolling through the data on her screen, she exhales relief. Tomás safely re-crossed the highway at 4 AM and has not moved since 5. He's asleep on a stomach full of soybeans in the tiny fragment of forest he tries to make home.

An hour later she's at an elementary school with a teammate who's sweating in a full-body tapir costume. Always children want to grab the dangling mini-trunk. They squeal when she holds out large seeds she's gathered from fecal samples. *When tapirs poop, they plant and fertilize trees*, she explains, *big trees, a long way from where they ate the seeds.* One boy says he knows how tapir meat tastes; her heart sinks. Will villagers stop poaching tapirs if their children love these gardeners of the forest?

All afternoon she and her team compile a report about roadkill on thirty-four highways built or widened for agribusiness. In three years, almost four hundred tapirs have died on these roadsides. Those are the reported ones. She's bent over many of the shattered bodies, stroking their ears. From a few she's carefully removed a GPS collar.

Driving home, tired, she hears the biting question buzzing again in her brain: *Am I helping save tapirs, or just documenting their extinction?* Vanished from two of Brazil's biomes, those of the Cerrado may be next.

Her headlights catch shadow on the road ahead. A tapir—Tomás? No, two, large and small, without collars, unknown to her. Stopped, she watches them cross into soybeans. The fleeting, certain sight of mother and child stills the bitter question, replacing it with another: *What intelligence, grit, and miracle keeps these ancient beasts alive in the world we've made?* It is beyond her, she knows. Buoyed, she drives on, picturing her team, their supporters around the world, and a new media campaign.

WEEK FOUR

The Poisoned

Golden Riffleshell Mussel

O n an early spring day in 2016, Indian Creek in Virginia coal country sparkled and skipped. Birds sang, insects chirred—and suddenly a few humans cheered. Standing in the creek they clustered around a man who cupped what looked like fuzzy stones. For weeks, the group had been looking for golden riffleshell mussels—specifically, gravid females. They had now found three.

With their treasures in a tub of water, they drove across the Kentucky border to a McDonald's parking lot. A malacologist in a van-made-traveling-lab met them. With a syringe he drew from the three mussels tens of thousands of larvae, called glochidia, each no bigger than a salt grain. The Virginia biologists hurried the adult females back to their creek bed, and the Kentucky malacologist carried their future to his lab.

In the shadows, behind this collaboration in hope, lay an ugly accident.

On August 27, 1998, a tanker truck overturned on Route 460 in Tazewell County, Virginia. Nearly 1,400 gallons of a chemical mixture used to manufacture foam rubber spilled into the Clinch River, just upstream from Indian Creek. Observers say the water went "snowy white." Nearly all creatures living in it perished, including half the golden riffleshells left on Earth.

One of them seems an insignificant thing, its hinged shell the size of a chicken's egg yolk. Scrub the fuzzy algae away and it's a similar color too, though fine jade-green rays shoot through its gold at precise intervals. Inside the bone-hard shell, a sheet of tissue, a mantle, wraps the animal's soft body. A tiny heart at its center synchronizes the mussel's organ rhythms, including a reproductive sequence that is one of the most intricate in all the animal kingdom.

The three females plucked from the bottom of Indian Creek that spring day had been brooding embryos in their gills since the summer before. When left in their creek bed, they're cued each spring to seduce certain small fish. Each female parts her shell and exposes her mantle, waggling its fingerlike protuberance. Seeing a delicacy—a minnow or insect larva—a fish swims in to snatch it. If the mussel determines this is a fish of the right species—a particular darter or sculpin—she snaps her shell closed, gripping his head. While he struggles, she squirts thousands of her offspring into his mouth and gills. These, the glochidia, then begin snapping to latch themselves onto gill-flesh. About four of every ten thousand succeed.

When the mussel releases him, the fish swims away bearing her children. For two to three weeks they glide with him and grow, fed by blood circulating through his gills, he no worse for the service. Then, grown to the size of peas, they let go—into a hospitable gravel bed if they're lucky—burrowing to make themselves invisible to mussel-eaters.

The Kentucky malacologist did not squirt the glochidia he took from the gravid females onto the gills of captive fish. That works with other mussel species, he's discovered, but not golden riffleshells. By trial and error he's developed a new way to grow them. While still in the McDonald's parking lot, he squirted the glochidia into petri dishes filled with serum extracted from rabbit blood. Then he drove these nursery-dishes to a carefully regulated room at his laboratory, and waited.

A century ago, golden riffleshells—and more than one hundred other mussel species—studded the beds of Indian Creek, the Clinch River, and all the other watercourses of the Upper Tennessee River Basin. More freshwater mussel species could be found there than any place on the planet. One didn't need to see them to know. A cupful of their clear water was evidence that these rivers sheltered robust mussel communities. Lying on the bottom, mussels filter particles from the water passing over them—particles that nourish them, and also pathogens, pharmaceuticals, acids, heavy metals, assorted toxins—purifying the water for all other water-dependent creatures, including humans.

Their vital service poisoned them. Half the mussel species once living in the Upper Tennessee River Basin are gone forever, or are apt to be. After sucking in decades of coal-mining, coal-burning, agricultural, and sewer contaminants, then the chemical spilled from the tanker truck, golden riffleshells became the rarest of the rare. By 2016, the last hundred or so held on at the bottom of Indian Creek.

Eighteen months after their rendezvous in the McDonald's parking lot, the Kentucky malacologist and the Virginia biologists waded into Indian Creek. Other biologists stood at two carefully chosen spots in the Clinch River. In bright mesh bags they carried seven hundred golden riffleshell mussels, grown in petri dishes and water tanks, midwifed to this moment by dozens of people in state and federal agencies, universities, and nonprofits who worked together, funded by nearly $4 million the trucking company agreed in court to pay. For nineteen years, their wild hope was this day.

Stooping in the shallows, water gurgling and glinting around them, the biologists tucked each golden riffleshell snugly into the gravel bed. They'd tagged and numbered their young charges with the hope of watching them grow for thirty, forty, even fifty years. They knew past odds. They knew that some of the mussels, cleansing the water for other river residents, would be poisoned. Maybe all. Humans at home in this watershed will decide how many. But for that bright September moment, scientists bound together in labor and love bent and blessed the small golden servants they hid at the bottom of the river.

Olm

Deep within the arid rock that bounds the eastern Adriatic Sea lies a dark kingdom. Though they hadn't been there, the area's human inhabitants knew of the kingdom long ago. A dragon rules it, they said, and they had proof. Going, after heavy rains, to the springs that gave them their drinking water, they found the dragon's babies washed up out of the deep. They quickly put the foundlings into streams, urging them to return to their mother underground where she guarded the fresh, sweet water of their life.

In the limestone mountains of Slovenia, Croatia, and Bosnia-Herzegovina, powerful rivers run through thickly forested gorges—then disappear, swallowed whole by the earth. Unseen, they snake through the porous rock, carving canyons, grottos, and caverns, pooling in lakes, plunging over cliffs, twisting, sinking, rising. Relentlessly the rivers push to new subterranean levels, leaving behind hollow labyrinths, some narrow as an arm, some vast as cathedrals. All dark as a grave.

Hidden from the world above, a pale creature lies still in the pools and lakes of these lightless caves. Its foot-long body, a slender cylinder, glows faintly pink—blood-filled capillaries tinting its thin, pigmentless skin. Pinker still are its external gills. Frilly little tufts colored with the blood pulsing through their transparency, they sprout at the back of a head shaped like a miniscule crocodile's. Add legs so tiny they seem fetal and a tadpole-like tail, and it's easy to see why people once called these creatures baby dragons.

The olm is in fact Earth's largest cave-dwelling animal. A salamander, it's unlike any other amphibian on the planet. Not only has it adapted to life in underground caves, but to life entirely underwater in underground caves—a double darkness. In this world apart, the olm lived tranquilly for one hundred million years. Except for heavy rains that washed a few away from home, humans might never have known of its existence.

What humans do know of the olm has largely come from aquarium-labs set up in three large caves, because the entrances to nearly all its home-caves are too small, too deep, too labyrinthine for researchers to reach. In the aquaria, captivated scientists ask this adaptive genius its secrets.

Left undisturbed, it rests in a near-death stillness. Shine a light, and it swims eel-like away. Not because it has seen the light. Eyes the olm is born with sink beneath its skin, sight proving useless for life in utter darkness. It swims away because its skin senses light—and it's an alien sensation. Settled again, it puts other more-than-human senses to work. With no visual cues for up or down or any direction, the olm tunes receptors in its head to signals from Earth's magnetic field. Once oriented, its inner ear picks up not only soundwaves in the water, but also in the ground. If it hears a slight displacement of water, its alerted nostrils sniff for precisely what sort of creature nears. Sensors in its snout then detect the bioelectric field that creature radiates and describe it to the waiting olm.

Always its finely tuned senses are asking, *Is it edible?* Cave waters deliver sporadically the tiny shrimp, crabs, and snails that olms eat. Not knowing when its next meal will wash in, an olm hoards its energy stores. It slows metabolism. Unless threatened, it moves slowly. If at all. In such slowed motion, an olm deprived of food can survive for a decade. Yes, a decade.

Neither is the creature in a rush to grow up. Its body takes fourteen full years to develop sexual organs and, even when adult, holds onto parts of its larva-body, like puny legs and external gills. It breeds maybe once every seven years. And though it weighs less than an ounce, an olm lives longer than an elephant—some as long as a century.

While fascinating, watching olms in aquaria doesn't tell researchers how they're doing at home. An intrepid few in wet suits strap on oxygen tanks to enter that other kingdom. Carefully roping themselves to the sunlit world, they lower themselves deep into cracks in the earth. They swim through passages no wider than their bodies and dive two, three hundred feet into liquid darkness lit only by a headlamp's beam. Dozens of scientists have been to outer space; only a handful to the heart of the olm universe.

And in this remoteness they find human waste. Waters that for millions of years have streamed and percolated through porous bedrock, shaping a world of fantastical caves, now pass first through mounds of factory waste, mining sludge, poorly treated sewage, garbage dumps, and fields sprayed with pesticides. The toxins in all of it the divers find far beneath the surface, in cave waters, and in the delicate pink tissues of olms. Some populations have disappeared; all are imperiled.

Nearly a million tourists each year stare at the wonders of Slovenia's massive Postojna Cave, including olms in an aquarium. They crowded close in 2016 when, in public view, a female olm laid eggs that hatched twenty-one baby olms. Few scientists and no ordinary citizens had before witnessed the laying or the hatching. News outlets around the world buzzed. Researchers fed the attention, hoping to transform popular dragon fantasies into real-life olm-awe, hoping awe would become fervor to protect olm-waters.

Which are human waters. Inhabitants of the land that arcs the eastern Adriatic Sea still get their drinking water from underground streams. This sinuous stream network is the great dragon. If the mother waters are poisoned, it is not only her baby dragons that will be poisoned. As people long ago knew, what befalls the dragon befalls all those who rely on her.

Laysan Albatross

In the day's first light he skims the surface, one wingtip tapping the tranquil sea. Suddenly he pivots into the wind and is lifted up, up. Soaring to fifty feet he peaks, banks leeward, and plunges downwind, down to surface-skim again, all without a single wingbeat. Over and over he plays this sequence, snow-white breast glowing in the morning sun.

"Dynamic soaring," engineers call his looping flight, which they study for its elegance and efficiency. It has carried him two thousand miles with barely a wingbeat. For three months he had been feeding in the Bering Sea. Then, in the first days of November, he felt a summons and set off, soaring night and day, a magnetic reckoning in his brain directing him to a tiny ring on the Pacific's vast azure expanse: Midway Island, remotest tip of the Hawaiian archipelago.

Fanning his six-foot wingspan, he sets down and begins a galumphing walk inland, passing hundreds of other albatrosses. He pays them little heed. The summons that has drawn him across the ocean impels him to one square yard of earth. Arriving, he points his bill straight up, stretches his neck its full length, and calls to the sky.

Every year he returns here, a stone's throw from where he hatched. And every year his mate meets him here. Gently they touch bills and settle into the grass. She tilts her head as he nibbles her cheek, his hooked bill softly rimming her eye.

Ringing their quiet reunion is a raucous dance party. Pairs of adolescent birds bill-snap and bob-strut, wing-lift and bill-tuck; they whinny, whine, clap their bills so fast they buzz, and rise up on tiptoes to moo at the sky. They eye each other intently, making up the dance as they go, each bird testing the other's ability to catch cues and synchronize moves. For eight months they'll dance, auditioning new partners. Next November they'll start over. The youngest dancers are three years old and will keep at this courtship ritual until they're six or seven. Once paired, a couple will spend another two years perfecting their dance—utterly unique to them—and their bond. Barring death they may be together for fifty years.

The long-bonded pair ignores the youngsters—and the rapt photographer, here to witness. Sure of each other, they have work to do. They quietly mate and preen each other, then eight days later scrape a shallow bowl in the earth where she lays one creamy, brown-speckled egg. For two months they take turns brooding their in-egg offspring, bending close and speaking to it. *Eh-eh*, they say.

When a downy gray chick finally breaks free, she knows them. She peeps—a greeting, and a plea. The male bill-strokes his new daughter then heads out to sea. To the baby's insistent peeping and probing bill, her mother opens hers and regurgitates a stream of greenish oil down the little throat, a meal she's been saving for this occasion. Then she tucks the downy squirmer beneath her and waits. The male returns a day or so later and opens his bill to the begging one. He's been feeding on small squid and fish eggs and coughs up a portion for the chick, then settles himself on the nest to begin his turn as sheltering parent. The female wheels out to sea.

For almost three weeks they will tag team, feeding and sheltering, never leaving their chick alone. The photographer records how she grows and grows. Her parents begin leaving her for short, then longer spells. She wanders, tossing sticks and bones into the air, waiting, hungrily.

Soon it takes both parents foraging continuously to feed her. They float on the surface at night, snapping up shininess. Squid are shiny on the night sea. So are fishing lures, cigarette lighters, golf balls, and plastic bottle caps. Nutritious fish eggs mass in shiny tangles of plastic fishing line. Laysan albatrosses swallow it all. Then they fly home and spill it into their babies' bellies.

Every cell of an albatross is made from the sea. They trust what it gives them. But the currents of the central Pacific, swirling between California and China, have been made a soup of cast-off plastic—billions of pieces that never completely decompose. Each year Midway's albatrosses unwittingly feed five tons of these pieces to their little ones.

 After months of plastic-laced meals, the chick slumps, lethargic. The trash in her stomach is stuck, taking up space. She feels full, but she's starving. Toxins in the plastics are leaching into her bloodstream. Helpless, her parents stop coming with food she refuses.

Every chick hatched with her on the island has plastic in its belly. At four months, the stronger ones cough up the junk in a bolus. When she tries, something sharp tears her soft gut membranes. The cleansed fledglings waddle to the shoreline. As they gallop into a stiff wind that lifts them over the sea in their first thrilling flight, she raises her head and gasps. *Eh-eh*, she tries to call.

After the long days of her dying, the photographer kneels and cradles her, whispering into the downy tuft on her head. *I'm sorry*. With scissors he cuts open her snow-white belly. He lifts out three bottle caps, a pocket-size doll, a comb, a printer cartridge, and random plastic shards. He scoops her gut cavity clean and in the hollow carefully arranges the plastics, creating a kind of shadow box.

His camera records her wrecked beauty. The shutter snaps and snaps, and then after, in the silence, he hears *Eh-eh, eh-eh*—thousands more dying chicks calling him to be their witness too.

Giant River Otter

The boy eases his canoe from the river into the creek mouth, skin tingling. Watching for sunken logs, he rounds a tight dogleg. Ululating screams ricochet off the forest wall, pelting him as several small cannonball-like heads charge the canoe, rush away, charge again, screaming, screaming. The boy's heart leaps and pounds but somehow remembers what he's been told. Easing the canoe backward, he coos—in otter. The screamers go quiet. They bob in the water like a row of periscopes, round eyes watching him. Droplets on the long whiskers rimming their faces grant them glinting halos in the morning sun.

With a whistle, one otter breaks the trance. Waked, the boy counts—five—as they pivot and glide quickly up the creek. He's met them on their morning fishing trip, not at the family's main campsite as he'd hoped. Wanting more to report, he ties the canoe and wades, searching the banks. Tracks show a pair were here with the sunrise, patrolling, scenting all campsites they've cleared along the creek with their claim.

Back in the village he tells the researchers who trained him and pay him as a scout about the otters' charge. They frown. Here in a pristine rainforest in Guyana they didn't expect otter-alarm. If never harmed, the gregarious creatures will swim close to boats, curious, inquiring. Hunters in the mid-1900s, offered large sums for their velvety pelts, shot them as they came, tens of thousands—until grieved citizens labored to change fur-trade laws. Now, maybe five thousand swim the watercourses of ten South American countries. In Guyana, with more untouched forests than any nation in Amazonia, fewer otters know humans. But that's changing.

The next day the boy ties the canoe before the dogleg. Imagining himself invisible, he threads his way along the bank opposite the otters' campsites. He walks and walks, watching for vipers, scorpions—till screams seize his heart. Dropping to a squat, he raises his binoculars.

Across the creek the family shrieks a reunion song, a gentler variation on yesterday's alarm chorus, a tone poem no other giant otter family sings. Two yearlings rush the adults, two clumsy cubs sputtering in their wake. The adults yield the catfish they've carried home to the babysitters, who clasp the fish between webbed forepaws. As they tear into their reward, the cubs wail at their older siblings to share.

Ignoring the ruckus, the grown otters clamber out of the water. The largest, his body as long as the boy's father is tall, plus the two-foot oar of his tail, waddles to the family latrine to leave a pungent signpost for passersby. The others follow his mate, their mother, onto a fallen log. She rubs her sinuous body against the warm bark, her three grown offspring shimmying in rapt imitation. Dry enough, they tangle themselves vying for the delicious spot nearest her. A son lands there, and she begins nibbling his ears. He is soon nibbling the sister pressed to his neck, and she, with a reach, draws the other brother into their grooming, cooing daisy chain. Still entwined, they doze in the midday sun. The yearlings tussle with the cubs, in and out of the water.

On the opposite bank the boy draws in a notebook the creamy shape birthmarked on each one's neck fur, shapes that identify them to other otters, and researchers. By their shapes he names them: Flame, Moth Wing, Crescent Moon. . . .

Half asleep in the sun he hears a lilting hum: *Let's go*. The matriarch is leading the way to the water for late-afternoon fishing. The youngsters clamor to come. She says no.

Taking the long route home, the boy hears clanging and whirring. He slips his canoe into tall weeds and creeps along the bank. Downriver he sees a boat sucking up riverbed through a huge hose and dumping it on the bank in heaps. Men toss shovelfuls of the mud into slanted troughs, then pour on water, and something else. Most of the sludge washes out. The rock bits left, other men take and burn in pans.

The gold rush sweeping Amazonia has invaded this forest. Thirty thousand men in Guyana alone, hungry for wages, have taken up small-scale mining—meaning they've taken up mercury. Pouring it onto river sediment to bond the gold in it, they wash mercury into the rivers and onto the soil. Refining the gold, they burn mercury into the air—thirty-eight tons every year sent into the earth, water, and air of this one country. The miners touch it, breathe it. All Guyanese who breathe air and eat fish also absorb the mercury—for generations after the miners have gone.

The researchers return the following year with someone new. He asks the boy's mother for a bit of hair, hers and her baby daughter's; it might explain why the little girl isn't walking yet. When the man wants to go fishing, the boy paddles him to the otter family's creek. While the scientist cuts samples from his catch, the boy wades the shallows. He sees something bobbing in a snag of branches, something he can't name until he's bending over it—an otter cub, eyes gone, flesh peeling away.

Maybe disease, something genetic, a stressed mother, the scientist hypothesizes. The boy looks away. *Or mercury poisoning*, he says. The man nods. *Maybe*.

The boy takes the bag he offers and gently slides the cub inside. The man promises he'll test the body. They paddle home without words until the boy slaps the canoe and says, *We scientists*—he gestures, including them both—*do we just collect samples of dead and dying things?* Looking at the trees, the sky, the water, the boy, the man answers, *Not anymore*.

WEEK FIVE

The Hunted

Chinese Pangolin

Somewhere in the silence after midnight she pokes her pink snout out of the burrow. She smells gentle rain. Pulling herself wholly out, she waits for the baby to get a firm purchase on her tail, then begins her slow night walk along the forest floor. Sometimes she toddles on two legs, forelimbs held to her chest. Down on all fours, she folds her front feet back, knuckle-walking to protect her curved, two-inch claws.

A short walk on, she stops, lifts her snout, sorting the scents, then rises onto her hind legs and pivots. The tail-riding pup holds tighter. She unfolds her front feet and lunges at a dirt mound, claws ripping it open. As termites explode from the crater she thrusts her head into their fury, closing her thick-lidded eyes, shutting off valves in her nostrils and ears while her supple, sticky tongue—more than a foot long—spins out of her mouth, slipping into every crevice of the nest. Defenders rush her body but bounce off the armor that shields all but her soft face and underbelly. A few bites there are a small price to pay for this rich meal.

Any medieval knight would have envied her armored suit. Overlapping scales—eighteen rows in variegated shades of bronze—protect the small anteater-like creature, and not only from termite bites. This Chinese pangolin shares her home in Nepal's Himalayan foothills with great cats. Should one reach for her, she will slide her baby to her belly and curl around it, an impenetrable ball not even a tiger's fangs can pierce. Her scales are keratin, the protein of human fingernails, and rhino horn. With this one defense the shy, toothless, slow pangolin, the world's only scale-covered mammal, has thrived for eighty million years.

Near dawn, weary and insect-sated, the mother shifts her attention. Finding a congenial bank, she puts her formidable digging tools to it, then twists her head like a drill bit to widen the hole. In less than five minutes she is three feet in and under, the entrance sealed up, the day's rest commenced.

Until it's broken by sharp cracks of sound one after another after another. She scoops her baby beneath her and rounds into her tiger-proof shield. The earth shakes and falls down around her. She can curl no tighter. Even with her snout pressed to the pup, she can smell the second they are exposed to open air—and to a new creature—no, two new creatures—whose odors jolt her every nerve.

The gloved man grabs the pangolin at the base of her tail. When he lifts her to drop her into a bag he grunts, pleased to see a pup fall away from her. He grabs and bags it, too. Then he unties the dog whose nose found the treasure and pats him on the head.

Once home the man sends his son with a message for the stranger. *Come after dark*. The strange man walked into their village a few days ago selling creams and lotions for the women. But he talked to the men about pangolins. Only a few of them have ever seen the rare creatures, but they mentioned that one of their own, away at school, studies them. The elders said that clever hunters used to capture pangolins. They brought bad luck to the village.

Waiting for dark, the man opens the bag and gazes at the fantastical animals, like none he has ever seen. Yes, he *is* a clever hunter. He will be rid of them before bad luck can find him, or the village. Making sure his son does not see, he pulls the pup from the mother and gives the little one to his wife to boil.

When the stranger appears and looks inside the writhing bag he smiles. He takes sixteen thousand rupees from his pocket. *More than twice what I would have paid two years ago*, he says. The hunter then offers a packet: scales boiled off the baby, earning him more rupees. Suddenly he wonders how he'll explain his new wealth in the village. Or hide it.

After stops in three more villages the pangolin trader arrives at a camp on the Tibet border with a pound of pangolin scales and six living pangolins. For each he receives double what he paid. Workers in the camp thrust tubes down the pangolins' throats and force-feed them limestone slurry. They inject water under the pangolins' skin. The creatures swell and go listless. Then they stuff the bloated animals into bags and pack them on mules through the mountains into China. Twice more the pangolins change hands, their price-per-bloated-pound doubling each time. The last hands slit the pangolins open at the throat and belly, then throw them into boiling vats.

In China's best restaurants, menus boast savory pangolin dishes, like pangolin-fetus stew. In medicine shops, traditional practitioners pulverize pangolin scales and prescribe them for psoriasis, poor circulation, asthma, anxiety, cancer. To meet the demands of appetite and illness, a Chinese pangolin, or one from the seven other pangolin species, is snatched from the wild every five minutes—more than two million in the last fifteen years. She is the world's most trafficked animal.

In the Himalayan village a young man comes home after years away at forestry school. He shows the elders and his neighbors pictures of pangolins. He tells them what remarkable creatures they are, a treasure hidden here in their forest, that they are disappearing, that he has money from the government to study and protect them. Will anyone help him find pangolins?

The hunter, who cannot sleep, who feels the eyes of the mother pangolin searching him every night says, *I will. I and my son.*

Ring-tailed Lemur

Clouds around the descending plane dissolve and the island rises out of the blue. Looking down, she imagines a tangled mass of plants—on it, a few primitive primates rafting across the channel from Africa, jumping onto the island-ark, and, for sixty million years, blooming wildly into a family tree of who-knows-how-many species of lemur, from gorilla-size to mouse-size, here and only here in all the world, on Madagascar.

She's lucky, she knows. Around the time of Christ humans also rafted here, and lemurs have been disappearing ever since. She's been invited to study one of the species left, one her advisor calls "tough as an old boot." Of the 750,000 ring-tailed lemurs that roamed Madagascar when she was born, about 2,500 hold on.

Another graduate student meets her in a beat-up Jeep. As they drive to the research site, a term from her ecology textbook pops into her mind all along the road. "Habitat fragmentation": swatches of forest hacked at for cookstove charcoal or slashed and burned for vegetable patches and cattle pasture. When they stop for gas she watches children play, kicking empty plastic bottles. The nation's grim poverty statistics take on flesh in their thin limbs and hollow cheeks. Would she deny their families vegetable patches for lemur habitat?

At the camp, a somber impromptu meeting mutes their arrival. Forestry students from the capital, surveying the area adjoining the reserve, have found a snare. The local men who form the reserve's monitoring team, whose villages gave the land for this research site, speak in clipped sentences. Killing and eating lemurs is *fady*, taboo, among their people. And, they believe, lemurs—attracting scientists and tourists—will better the lives of their children.

The next morning she's assigned to shadow the monitoring team's lemur expert. He tells her the snare is the work of outsiders. Probably their children are hungry—as were his, before the reserve hired him. In the gallery forest along the river he points to a clearing.

Twelve creatures the size of house cats sit, heads lifted, looking east. A female, baby on her shoulder, anchors them—mothers with infants, then younger females radiating from her center. Four males accept the periphery. The lemurs' long striped tails lend balance as they lean back, legs splayed, arms open and palms up, baring their white bellies to the rising sun. Nights can be cold in the desert of Madagascar's far south, and their bodies speak the pleasure of their morning warming ritual.

At a soft *hmm* from the matriarch, the troop rouses. She, the other mothers, plus one male they designate, lead the procession to breakfast, tails lifted like banners. Along the way, the males scrape a thorny spur grown on their wrists against saplings, leaving scent. Females perform handstands, rubbing their scented bottoms on trees. When other lemurs pass by later, they'll read the troop's biographies: sex, age, genetics, virility, fertility, illness, stress. Complex bouquets—more than two hundred scent compounds—and twenty-eight nuanced calls make each ring-tail a pointed communicator.

Giving little attention to their human attendants, the troop arrives at a large tamarind tree. Most of its pods have dropped to the ground. But a few succulent ones dangle above. The matriarch and her ladies-in-waiting leap into the branches to claim them while the others forage among the fallen. Discontent, the favored male creeps warily up the trunk toward a tastier meal. A scolding cackle erupts and the nearest female, infant clinging, lunges at his insolence, cuffing him on the ear, forcing retreat.

For all the times he's seen this, the lemur monitor laughs with the novice researcher. They follow when the troop withdraws to a glade for the midday siesta and watch each ring-tail rake the furred body of another with lower teeth ridged like a comb. The air buzzes softly with lemurs humming and purring their bond.

For the budding scientist the days pass in data collection. Meaning feces collection. She assumes the samples will reveal the lemurs' gut parasites. Her advisor says yes, that, but also routes of the illegal pet trade. Comparing the DNA of their samples with samples collected at lemur rescue centers will show whether ring-tails are being taken from this area. If people are hunting lemurs here, they're likely selling babies snared with their mothers. A baby sold for two dollars pays what most workers earn in three days. Taken from their troop, fed alien foods, more than half the little ones die. Often survivors, lunging and biting in desperation, are killed.

Her research season ended, she rides to the capital with some forestry students. They're celebrating jobs offered to them in other villages that are now setting aside forest reserves because they see the possibilities and hope the wild can bring.

When they stop for a drink at a hotel bar, she wanders to the pool deck, smiling at the memory of the whole troop of wild lemurs sunbathing together. Two women ask the groundskeeper to take their photo. One holds out a cookie, and when a young ring-tail wearing a sequined collar jumps onto their table and snatches it from her hand, they smile. The shutter clicks.

She hurries back inside to her Malagasy friends. *A ring-tail on the deck, an illegal pet. Shouldn't we report it?*

They shrug. *Lemurs bring the hotel tourists, and tourist dollars help pay police.*

As her plane, muffled in clouds, climbs, she closes her eyes. Again, the image of the collared, harried lemur leaps into her mind. Through tears she sends social-media messages to her world-traveling friends: *Visit lemurs in their wild homes, not hotels.* She attaches a picture of her troop curled together under the trees. She tries to hear them purring.

Black Rhinoceros

He sits in the shade of a mopane tree, looking up at its butterfly-shaped leaves. *Rest*, his boss told him. But he remembers: It's his first day as a national park ranger and his trainer is showing him pictures. White rhino, black rhino—same shade of gray. Look at the lip, he learns—black rhino's is hooked. That two kinds of rhinoceros range South Africa surprises him. Growing up on the park's edge, he avoided the bush and its beasts. Life was precarious enough. This good job is going to ask a lot of him.

Sooner than he likes they're crouching in the bush. The training ranger has chosen a particular black rhino bull to follow, one he knows has spent the night nearby. Six months ago, he was on the team that tranquilized and felled the massive animal. Drilling a hole in the bull's smaller back horn, they embedded a radio transmitter to pulse its whereabouts—on or off its rightful owner. Before injecting the antidote, the team vet patched the hole beyond detection.

Following a path of trampled grass, the two men sight the rhino napping beneath a great mopane tree, a red-billed oxpecker perched and picking ticks from the thick wrinkles of his neck. The ranger points to a smaller tree ahead. Careful to stay downwind, they creep forward. *Chee-cheee*, the oxpecker warns her host. The men lunge into the tree as the creature heaves his bulk up and trots toward them—then stops, peering into the tall grass. The small dark marbles of his eyes see the men as merely another shadow on the savannah. Compensating, his calla lily-shaped ears swivel almost full circle. To the novice's horror, the senior ranger snorts in pitch-perfect rhino. The swiveling ears snap forward, locking on their target. Then the behemoth charges, his thundering hooves sending spears of panic through the new ranger's heart. He hears himself shout, *Shoot, shoot!*

Eight feet from their tree, finally able to see who roused him, the rhino brakes. He is twice as long as the young man is tall and twenty times his weight, and he is pawing the ground, snorting explosively. *See the delicate feathers fringing his ears, the beaky upper lip, the battle scars?* his superior instructs. Gazing at each other, both species calm. Smiling, the senior ranger drops his hat. The rhino sniffs it, then catches it on his long front horn and tosses it over his back. With a dexterity defying the physics of his size, he spins and races away, huffing like a steam engine.

Washed with relief, the young ranger laughs and laughs. Such speed and agility and impishness! He names the rhino Rasta, after his favorite rugby player. In the weeks that follow he sees that far from being sulky loners and bullies to a one, each black rhino is, like Rasta, a unique personality.

On nights of the full moon he works overtime, assigned to an area plagued by poachers slinking across the border from Mozambique. Black rhinos are extinct there. Of the one hundred thousand that roamed Africa in 1960, only 2,500 were left on the continent two decades ago. Now he's proud of all that South Africa has done to help double that number. But demand from Southeast Asia for the small number of rhino horns left on Earth—and their black-market price—has surged. The promised wealth wrecks many ordinary citizens' inner restraint.

To everyone's relief, this full-moon night passes with no detected violence. He naps and is reporting for his day shift when word comes from radio control that a horn is moving rapidly—too rapidly for a rhino—toward the park border. An armed unit speeds off to intercept the pulsing horn and its violators. He and a dog-ranger team are sent to find the carcass. The radio officer confirms they are looking for Rasta.

The dog lunges, pulling the men to a pool of blood. But no body. Running on, the dog suddenly stops, ears pricked. Inching forward they see Rasta in a field, wobbling, heaving. Each breath spurts blood from two holes in his skull. With a dose of opioids potent enough to fell him but not kill him, poachers butchered his face and left him. Cursing viciously, the young ranger sights Rasta's massive beautiful mutilated head. And puts three bullets in it. Then he leans against a thorn tree and sobs.

He is given time off, told to rest—then abruptly called back. His boss insists he visit Zambia with the project director of the North Luangwa Conservation Programme. As she drives, the director tells the ranger the story of five black rhinos arriving at Luangwa on a Hercules aircraft in 2003, gifts from his park to resurrect Zambia's extinct population. Almost fifty strong now, not one has fallen to a poacher.

He is silent, then says, *The killers, the syndicate kingpins, the people who think horn cures them, the men who carry it to look important—I hate them all.*

I know, she says. After a long pause she adds, *They have never been in a rhino's presence.*

He remembers: neither had he, before Rasta.

When they arrive, the project director introduces him to a smiling Zambian man about to board a bus with twenty squealing schoolchildren for a three-day field trip into the park. The Zambian sketches his story: A local farmer, he became a ranger at Luangwa, then started teaching children about rhinos in schoolrooms. *Which I still do*, he says. *But the rhinos are our best teachers. We bring children into their presence.*

Hawksbill Turtle

Six women stand waist-deep in the sea, their skirts floating around them like flower petals. Holding the hundred-pound turtle at the surface, they each, in turn, lay a hand on her amber-streaked carapace. Then the oldest woman nods, and, in unison, they let her go. As the turtle dives, a single soprano rises, a song to bless her perilous way.

The female hawksbill swims across the channel to the next island. When night falls, she hauls her bulk again onto that shore and again begins the slog through sand. She was here last night, feeling her way to a nesting place, when three men surrounded her and lifted her into a boat and sped her to the other island. There they laid her on a board, and while one held a towel over her salt-crusted eyes and massaged her neck, another glued a cell-phone-size box to her shell. When the glue was dry, they called for the mothers to carry her to the sea.

It is the box, with its blinking orange light and bobbing antenna, that tells the men she has returned to the island where they found her. Missing from most area maps, this mere smudge of sand in the Solomon Islands is the magnetic center of her inner map. Quiet for decades, now it thrums. Its pulse drew her out of the Great Barrier Reef and pulled her across a thousand miles of the South Pacific, past scores of other sandy islands, compelling her to keep on—*Not that one*—keep on, thirty days, forty days, until it signaled, *Here!*

Here thirty years ago she broke from an egg beneath a full moon. Dozens of other inch-long hatchlings clambered around her, over her, all of them together pushing out of their sandy womb and scrambling with her down the beach, looking for the moon's liquid reflection to direct them to the sea. Slower ones were snatched at daybreak by gulls and crabs. Those that made water's edge surrendered themselves to currents that swept them in arcs and gyres out to the deep, into the path of diving seabirds and gliding sharks. Some escaped, and were entangled in fishing nets or plastic bags and six-pack rings. A few survived two years, three years. Finding themselves alive and adult, they began a life of foraging along reefs, hunting especially for sponges, plucking them from crevices in the coral with their raptor-like beaks. Few animals and no other turtles can eat sponges, whose bodies are full of glass needles. Sponges starve corals. Cleaning them from the coral streets, hawksbills protect the sprawling city that shelters millions of creatures.

Of every thousand hawksbill hatchlings, one will survive to breeding age. The female dragging her three-foot shell up the dark beach is that one. She groans. The sand is heavy and strange. She hasn't left the water since she entered it under moonlight here thirty years ago. Difficulty and strangeness cannot deter her, though. She knows nothing of doubt or hesitation. She labors on beyond the tide's reach till she finds her place, hidden in beach grass. With her back flippers she digs a hole and into it drops a hundred or so soft, ping-pong-ball-size eggs. Quickly she covers them. Only then does she allow herself a little rest.

A stone's throw down the beach two men wait. They see the dark blot of her shape and atop it a pulse of orange light. Those who put the light there have alerted this pair to the turtle's location. All of them lose sleep for her. Because a few nights ago, when a stalled boat kept the ranger pair at sea, other men slipped their boats ashore. Sweeping the beach with flashlights they found another one-in-a-thousand survivor laboring through the sand. They waited until the turtle mother had laid her eggs. Then, when she made the turn toward home, they set on her with machetes. She too wore a GPS tracker, which the poachers hacked off and hurled into the sea.

It is illegal in the Solomon Islands to kill a nesting sea turtle. It is illegal in most nations to buy or sell or export any sea-turtle product. Still, the poachers have customers waiting for her savory meat, and for her eggs, said to be an aphrodisiac. Peeled from her body, carved and polished, her shell will become the gleaming tortoiseshell combs and bracelets, earrings and belt buckles people around the globe covet. It's a primal impulse: putting her body on or into our own, we wish to absorb the force and radiance of so fiercely determined a creature.

The rangers guard the light slowly blinking its way back down the beach. When this turtle mother eases into the sea's embrace, they exhale relief, then resume their patrol, protecting the eggs it has taken her three decades to lay. Will they see her in seven years, when she's ready to lay again? They can protect her here, but this island is a pinprick on the map of her vast and increasingly perilous journey. And it may be gone in seven years. Climate change is causing seas to rise in the Solomons at more than double the global average. Nearby islands have disappeared. Her birthplace, their birthplace, may be the next to slip under the waves.

The men know that. But beneath that fact, from each hawksbill heaving herself out of the sea and plodding up the sand, they feel a thrum, indescribable and unrelenting. Through the night, keeping watch, they hear themselves hum—her song, the women's song, a song of fierce devotion to those waiting to be born.

HOLY WEEK

The Desecrated

Bonobo

An ancient river curves across the belly of Africa, its vast green basin birthing, over the ages, a riot of life forms, including our closest kin. A million years ago the river deposited a sediment-bridge for some of these apes to cross, then dissolved it. Far- and near-shore siblings, separated, became different creatures.

As light wakes the Congo River's south bank, one cluster of treetops suddenly shakes as if touched by an intentional wind. From nests of woven branches rise what look like fifty chimpanzees, but slender, their legs longer, heads smaller, with faces black rather than chimpanzee-pink. Some move among nests offering kisses and intimate greetings. Some lie back, reaching fistfuls of leaves for breakfast in bed. Mothers suckle sleepy babes. Gradually, groups of ten or twelve swing off into the rainforest. When the alpha male of the last group left screams the signal to move out, the slow-to-wake alpha female—his mother—doesn't budge. He may be the general, but she is the queen. When she's ready, her group too leaps through the canopy in search of something especially delectable.

The ancestors of these apes—the ones marooned on the far side of the river—competed with gorillas for food and turned into fiercer creatures: chimpanzees. On this riverside—gorilla-less, well provisioned—their energies could take less turbulent channels. The creatures they became do fight, but bonobos will not kill one another. Led by females, they settle their conflicts with pleasurable touch.

The late-movers soon hear a message on the morning air. Pausing, they tilt their heads and listen to a precisely ordered sequence of bonobo calls describing the delectability ahead. Then they're off, crashing toward a patch of junglesop trees where a group of early-movers is feasting. Though there's been an invitation, though the fruit hangs thick, some pickings are richer, and who gets them must be settled. The newly arrived females approach their female hosts, arms open. Pairs embrace, rubbing the swollen pink cushions of their genitals together. Soon it's food that's being shared; in their etiquette of touch, everyone eats. Satisfied, the groups part for midday naps.

Some are sleepier than others. An adolescent male lies on his back on a broad log, feet in the air balancing a baby. She is not his sister, and her mother dozes in the branches above. He jiggles his legs, bouncing the babe, and when she grins he reaches up and tickles her back. She laughs and laughs, drawing the glance of an old female playing with sticks in a rivulet. No reason to intervene. Unlike chimp mothers, vigilant for violence against themselves and their young, bonobos need fear none in their group.

Still, there are rules. When another wide-awake adolescent male pesters a grown male to play, the youngster is sent tumbling. One wounded cry and his mother swoops in, screaming, two allies close behind, chasing the offender—until met by *his* mother and her allies. A male bonobo never leaves home; all his life he looks to his mother for status and defense. Leaving at puberty, females make new homes among strangers not by shrinking before males, but by crafting friendships with females. These now screaming the righteousness of their sons end their confrontation with caresses.

A man has witnessed and recorded all this. After the groups have reunited at their night nests, he walks home. It takes an hour. When he was a boy he woke to bonobos outside his window. Then civil wars brought waves of fighters careening through his village. Poor, unmoored, they committed horrors; among the many, they killed bonobos, honored forest kin. When war began to ebb, elders told the old stories—bonobos sharing food with the ancestors, leading lost ones home—and urged villages to unite and protect their forest. *Bonobos help us*, they said, *we help bonobos*.

Their Bonobo Peace Forest project has drawn scientists—who employ this man to observe the apes—as well as journalists, nonprofits, some tourists. Now his children go to school and to a clinic when they're sick. His wife has a sewing machine and her women's association makes clothing. Once a month he helps her take bundles of dresses and skirts to market. He won't let her go alone in this country many call the most dangerous on Earth for a woman.

While she bargains, he wanders the alley behind the bushmeat stalls, scanning faces. Transporters loiter near bicycles stacked with empty baskets, pockets full of cash. Three days ago, deep in the rainforest, they bought hundred-pound loads of meat from hunters slung with assault rifles and colonial-era guns left around after various wars. If the antelope, bush pigs, and monkeys didn't die in their snares, the hunters shot or clubbed them, then smoked them to withstand the long trip to market. It's a dangerous business. But hunters and transporters alike risk it over the poverty that gnaws 90 percent of their neighbors.

Another bicycle clatters in, delayed along the way. Its rider yells for help, and the bonobo observer steps up. It is not the son of his who slipped away into this grim trade, but it could be. Offloading quickly the smoke-darkened meat, he can't distinguish its type—until he lifts from a backpack a basket of charred hands and feet. Even this late in the market day and illegal, the bonobo delicacies will be snatched up.

Heartsore, the man gropes for something more to unload and notices the backpack has moved—on its own. He grabs the pack and runs. Tracking bonobos has made him strong and fast. When he can no longer hear curses behind him, he stops. Staring at his own hands, he reaches into the pack. The orphan inside reaches back.

Atlantic Bluefin Tuna

He began life the size of an eyelash, floating in the warm womb of the Mediterranean Sea. Thirty million eggs his mother spilled into the salty tumult. Against the odds he hatched, he survived, he grew into the natural miracle of his kind, called by many the king, the ultimate fish.

Now fully mature, he moves through the enormity of the open Atlantic. His back and flanks variegated blues, belly a silver iridescence, all of him flashed with gold, he is ocean light enfleshed. Ocean fluidity too. His is the most hydrodynamic shape on the planet, a streamlined perfection for great boundary-crossing migrations. Within, as well, he is made for distance travel: high hemoglobin concentration, quick oxygen uptake, and a greater percentage of red-muscle fiber than any other fish. For this dense, red flesh there is a grave price on his head.

With a small school he swims north, a translucent window at the top of his head funneling light to particles that read Earth's magnetic field. Infallible, this guidance system leads the bluefin to waters that can satisfy his muscular hunger. Off the coast of Norway his superior vision sights mackerel and herring. All but two of his twenty-one fins and finlets drop into neat slots flawlessly flush with his body and he rockets through the water forty miles-per-hour fast.

He eats and grows, grows and eats—almost any creature in the sea. For some, he plunges more than half a mile and sixty Fahrenheit degrees below body temperature.

His capacity to abide chilling dives or Mediterranean-to-Scandinavian swims comes from a *rete mirabile*, a "wonderful net" of veins and arteries interlaced. In the net's weave, blood chilled when frigid water rushes into his gills quickly heats. In a numb world, he is warm. Warm, his mind, his responses, are nimble and keen.

Come fall, he and his school cross the North Atlantic to forage off Nova Scotia. As the days shorten, they slide south. When the season turns, they turn too—north again to spots they remember as lush with fish. Simply gliding with the seasons along Atlantic coasts, in thirty years he could become a three-quarter-ton giant.

But his life is more than his own. In late spring, he is seized by an irresistible urge to return to the waters where he woke. Rich feeding grounds lose their allure. He and the school set out across the open ocean with a single, fierce focus.

Two thousand years ago, people stood on promontories to watch bluefin tuna pour through the Straits of Gibraltar. By the millions, the tuna came home to the Mediterranean to spawn. Now one of the world's most overfished species, bluefin are too few to be seen from the highlands. But there are other ways to watch for them.

On a calm July morning, a spotter plane circling the sapphire waters off Sicily radios a purse seine boat: *We got tuna!* Racing to the location, the boat encircles the school with a conical, mile-long net. Crew then begin cinching the net's bottom, like a drawstring purse closing around coins. One trapped mind in the water, the tuna spin a clockwise gyre—except the largest. He darts forward and back, then leaps, terror's rush intensifying his brilliant hues.

A tugboat towing an underwater cage draws alongside the imprisoning net. Divers jump in among the fish, open a gate, and herd them into the cage. Fear-crazed, the tuna obey. A diver surfaces and signals, *One, huge!* The boat crew hand him a pistol.

By the time they get the big bluefin onto the boat, the light has gone out of his black eyes. Three red circles bloom between them. Though his silver-blue iridescence too has begun to fade, the men standing around him can see themselves mirrored in the sheen of his skin. One stabs his side, releasing a hiss of air and steaming blood. Working quickly, the crew gut him and pack him with ice in a pine box. While the caged tuna will be towed to the coast, transferred to pens, and fattened for months, this exceptional bluefin will be flown to Tokyo and laid on the fish market's auction floor tomorrow morning. The men who live by fishing thump each other. *Thirty thousand dollars for sure!*

In the predawn dark the auctioneer rocks and cries numbers in a hypnotic singsong. Rolling little balls of flesh between their fingers, bidders assess texture and luster. The world's appetite for bluefin sushi and sashimi has been perfected here. It's said the best chefs can taste how afraid the fish was when he died. For a few bites of the finest bluefin belly their customers will pay hundreds of dollars.

Because this flesh is so coveted, those who have built an industry selling it pressure the committee that sets fishing quotas to let them take more and more endangered bluefin from the sea. Whatever number they're allowed, some take more—all told, perhaps double the quota.

It was not always so. Five generations ago, no culture craved bluefin belly. In Japan, if it was eaten at all, it was first buried for days to mellow the flavor. In North America, bluefin inadvertently caught were sold for pet food. Tastes can change.

But on this day the giant caught off Sicily is sold and hauled to a butchering table. The fishmonger cleans the body's long length. He selects a knife from his array. A master of his craft, he painstakingly slices the energy-rich flesh into thin strips, speaking solemnly to what he knows was a great fish.

African Elephant

The cacophony of snarled traffic stops when the pneumatic door shuts. Inside the shop's glass cases creamy white objects gleam: exquisitely carved chess sets and pendants, statues of Buddha, the Goddess of Mercy, and bearded men bearing scrolls. Shelves along the wall display less expensive bangles and talismans. Though ivory sales are illegal in this Vietnamese tourist center, and most of Asia, the shop is full. A young woman gazes at the most polished pieces. Her beloved must have the best.

Above its majestic blue shoulders, Kilimanjaro is shrouded in clouds. On the plain a family paces, kicking up red dust. At dusk on a blessedly ordinary day they would be processing slowly toward the low hills, their night shelter, bathed in the radiance of an ordinary twilight. Like yesterday's.

Just yesterday they passed hours in an emerald oasis where underground streams flowing from the great mountain bubble up. Between feedings in the lush vegetation they visited pools to drink and cool their dust-crusted hides. And meet friends. Wading into the water, they greeted another companionable family with rumbles and pirouettes, grasping trunks and putting them in each other's mouths, clicking tusks, ears spread like sails and flapping. A fearful little one wrapped his trunk around his mother's tusk. Floating beside her in the happy mayhem, he watched and learned this: *Our lives are twined together*.

At her signal, the dozen members of the family nudged the youngest up the pool's slick sides and followed their matriarch across the plain. In her prime at forty-five, she has led her family to food and water when the land cracked with drought. She has lost none of the little ones born to them, so keen is her sense of their natural predators' craft. The matrix of her mind hums with a deep understanding of this place. Other families know this and take cues from her movements.

She's had to alter those movements utterly. As a calf following her mother she learned roads elephants had trod for centuries, crossing the continent. At large watering holes her family reveled in a herd of hundreds. In her lifetime humans on Kilimanjaro's plains have killed 90 percent of her community. Those left live as refugees in refuges too small for their enormous bodies and minds.

In yesterday's blessedly ordinary dusk, before leading her family into the night hills, she stopped to let the children play. The older calves dropped to the ground, an invitation. Rushing them, the babies piled on. Their mothers and aunties encircled them, touching rumps, touching trunks and tusks, talking in low rumbles. Family members absorb their matriarch's manner, and this one is known among elephants for gentleness.

But this day's dusk is neither ordinary nor blessed.

The morning slid open with its usual beauty. Descending the hills, fresh and cool, the family began to trot, smelling the deliciousness of the oasis. Their matriarch sent them ahead, herself keeping pace with a calf limping from a fall into a garbage pit. Until a gunshot shattered the soft light. Struck in the chest, the matriarch stumbled forward, shoving her calf roughly toward the sisters who turned back to her, trumpeting, *Run!*

When she fell to her knees, the poachers swarmed in and emptied an AK-47 into the back of her head. With axes they hacked off her face below the eyes. They fled with two fifteen-pound tusks, leaving four tons of flesh to rot. Her severed trunk, with its tender, fingery tips, lay limp in the dust.

As this desecrated dusk collapses into night, her oldest daughter dares to approach. Glands behind her eyes stream and she groans softly. Coming to the body, she runs the tips of her trunk gingerly over the whole, then lingers where the part she knew best—her mother's mouth and soft tongue—lie garbled. In a huddle, the others inch forward. Their trunks wave, touching their own faces for comfort, glands at their temples streaming. All of them trunk her tortured flesh. Some then walk a short distance, and look away. Others nudge her with their feet, gently or roughly. One sister rocks back and forth, the limping calf hidden beneath her, sucking his trunk like a thumb.

For two days, the oldest daughter stands over her mother's body. Hyenas bed nearby. Then, dehydrated, she leaves, joining other family members on the worn paths of their routine, as trauma survivors do.

Quickly the mountain of flesh disappears, feeding the lives of others. They leave behind her skull. For weeks her family returns, smelling, tasting, caressing the one who was their well-being. In rumbling groans below human hearing they tell their distress to all the elephants of the plain. The low-frequency sounds ripple through the ground into elephant feet, which turn toward the place of her dying. Families come and touch, acknowledging a great leader is gone.

Among the elephants at the place of her slaughter are humans who also knew the matriarch's greatness. They come and weep, and the elephants feel their grief.

—————

The young woman leaves the shop glowing with her purchase. She doesn't know that during the hour she was inside, poachers hacked the tusks off three elephants to sell to a pyramid of middlemen to sell to cartels who supply shops like the one she's leaving. For their incisor teeth, carved and polished, seventy-two African elephants a day, twenty-five thousand a year, are slaughtered. What the woman in love knows is that the ivory carving she's purchased for her new husband will show him to be a man of standing and good taste, sensitive to beauty and their culture, the best sort of man.

Takhi

The last wild one vanished from human sight in 1969. Mongolian herders saw him like a mirage far off in the yellow hills. And then they didn't. Though to Western science his kind didn't exist until 1878, the nomads knew him as ancient and immortal. He was untamable, progenitor of the horses that made their lives possible. Science named his species after the man who delivered a skull and hide for analysis: "Przewalski's horse." To the Mongolians living at the edges of his realm, he and his kind had always been *Takhi*. Spirit.

In a land of extremes, herds of takhi thrived for tens of thousands of years. Perhaps because the nomads believed them immortal, they drove ever larger flocks of sheep and goats into spirit-horse grasslands. When Europeans and Americans got news of the only horses never tamed for human use, they wanted them. Expeditions captured takhi foals by shooting the uncapturable stallions and mares. Held in circuses and zoos, takhi young died. In the end, twelve survived.

The last free takhi had vanished when a nineteen-year-old Swiss woman saw wild horses painted on the walls of caves in southwestern France. Their haunting beauty, stroked on stone by prehistoric artists, touched her, as did her realization that all the animals—aurochs, ibex, bison, bears—leaping among the horses had disappeared from that landscape. She went to see takhi enclosed in a zoo. Her sadness seeded a dream.

Fifteen years earlier, in the mid-1950s, a few conservationists had decided to devote themselves to the last captives. They began a careful breeding program with the twelve surviving in the Munich and Prague zoos. Encircled in their attentiveness, the takhi multiplied and multiplied. By the early 1990s, zoos and parks in thirty-three countries tended 1,500 horses.

At that moment, the Swiss woman was ready. Since seeing them painted on cave walls and penned in a zoo, she had given herself to wild horses, learning everything known about them. In 1993, she selected six stallions and five mares born in the captive breeding program and brought them to a protected plateau in the south of France, land that echoed their ancestral home. Though experts warned against it, she released the zoo-raised animals to run freely and form their own societies. Some had never grazed grass. A decade later, the little band of eleven had swelled to fifty-five horses that remembered who they were. Aggression among them had ebbed; stallions no longer killed foals.

It was time to begin taking takhi home.

Twelve were coaxed into small crates. In the hold of a cargo plane the woman and her team sat among the crates for the forty-five-hour flight, feeding the animals apples and hay, singing and telling them stories. When they landed on the remote steppe in western Mongolia, a crowd of herding people met them. Some who remembered spirit horses from their childhoods had ridden their tamed horses more than a hundred miles to see takhi again. Most rode to see them for the first time.

The crates were lined up on the windswept steppe. Smelling the wild, the horses neighed and pawed the wooden floors. Elders poured a blessing of mare's milk over each impatient captive. Then, in unison, men perched on the top of each crate lifted slats that set the takhi free. Above the sound of hooves pounding away from them, men, women, and children clapped and cheered and wept. *Thank you*, they said, *thank you*.

Other takhi lovers have brought horses home to two more places in the Mongolian wilderness. Across the border, Chinese conservationists protect a herd, as do Ukrainians, Kazaks, and Russians on expanses of steppe they've fought wars to call their own. Across their ancient homelands as many as two thousand takhi run and live wild lives. A herd flourishes in the one-thousand-square-mile Chernobyl Exclusion Zone, evacuated and declared a dead zone after a nuclear reactor exploded in 1986. Once extinct in the wild, takhi are now designated simply "endangered."

This is good, but it's only the beginning, the takhi woman says of her dream. *We want not just to bring takhi home. We want them to live on for six million years.*

Golden lion tamarins and brown pelicans, bald eagles and peregrine falcons, red wolves, gray wolves, Florida panthers, California condors, and Vancouver Island marmots, the nene, the bontebok, the addax, American burying beetles and American alligators, yellowfin madtoms and piping plovers. All these species and more once seemed certain to vanish from the earth. And all have returned—some astoundingly, some haltingly—because humans, many or few, allowed a wild hope to bloom.

In such as these, a dream, seeded in sadness and love, quietly defies cynicism and grows by turning fear into work. Their dream-work is daily, tedious, and life-giving. It calls up the body's strength and the mind's capacity; it stretches the soul with listening to those the dream threatens, daring to ask them and others for help. Dream-workers lie awake with doubt and sit still when set back. They go on again, more clear eyed, their love refined by the One Undying Love that animates all things.

Through such as these, the wild-not-impossible hope deep within each of us is born again and again into the world. Love takes flesh and makes all things new.

AFTERWORD

The stories in these short chapters are merely sketches. All of these animals live lives infinitely more intricate and magnificent than I can describe in this limited space. Short as these stories are, I hope they've inspired in you wonder and grief. Questions too, like: *How far do elephant rumbles travel through the ground? Has white-nose syndrome spread to bats in my hometown? Where on Delaware Bay can I see red knots feeding?* and especially, *What can I do to help?*

Professional scientists and citizen scientists, conservationists, paid and volunteer, are daily discovering more about the species they love. Some of the information in this book, true when I included it, will have changed by the time you read it. At the websites below, species lovers gladly share what they know, what they're searching to know, and what they're doing to protect these creatures. Many also have social-media platforms where they post updates of their lives with animals. As you come to know these animal protectors, my prayer is that you catch their wild hope.

This portion of the book is duplicated on the Paraclete Press website, at www. paracletepress.com/wildhope, where the links may be followed easily with a click.

SUMATRAN ORANGUTAN

World Wildlife Fund's Bukit Tigapuluh Project: https://www.worldwildlife.org/projects
/thirty-hills
The Orangutan Project: https://www.orangutan.org.au
Orangutan Foundation International: https://orangutan.org
Orangutan Land Trust: http://www.forests4orangutans.org

RED KNOT

American Bird Conservancy: https://abcbirds.org

Atlantic Flyway Shorebird Initiative of the National Fish and Wildlife Foundation: https://www.nfwf.org/amoy/Pages/home.aspx

Birdlife International: https://www.birdlife.org/worldwide/partnership/about-birdlife

The Audubon Society: https://www.audubon.org

AMUR LEOPARD

Wildlife Conservation Society, Russia: https://russia.wcs.org/en-us

Wildcats Conservation Alliance: https://conservewildcats.org

GALAPAGOS PENGUIN

Center for Ecosystem Sentinels: https://ecosystemsentinels.org

Galapagos Conservancy: https://www.galapagos.org

STAGHORN CORAL

Coral Restoration Foundation: https://www.coralrestoration.org

The SECORE Foundation: http://www.secore.org/site/home.html

Coral Restoration Consortium: http://reefresilience.org/restoration/restoration-introduction/coral-restoration-consortium

PANAMANIAN GOLDEN FROG

Panama Amphibian Rescue and Conservation Project: http://amphibianrescue.org

Amphibian Ark: http://www.amphibianark.org

INDIANA BAT

Bat Conservation International: http://www.batcon.org

White-Nose Syndrome Response Team: https://www.whitenosesyndrome.org

National Wildlife Federation: https://www.nwf.org/About-Us

KOALA

Australian Koala Foundation: https://www.savethekoala.com

Friends of the Koala: https://www.friendsofthekoala.org

Port Macquarie Koala Hospital and Conservation Foundation: https://www.koalahospital.org.au/act-now/conservation-foundation

BLACK-FOOTED FERRET

The Nature Conservancy: https://www.nature.org/en-us/explore/animals-we-protect/black-footed-ferret

Black-footed Ferret Friends: http://blackfootedferret.org

Defenders of Wildlife: https://defenders.org/black-footed-ferret/basic-facts

MONARCH BUTTERFLY

Journey North: https://journeynorth.org/monarchs

Monarch Joint Venture: https://monarchjointventure.org

Monarch Watch: https://www.monarchwatch.org

NORTH ATLANTIC RIGHT WHALE

Center for Coastal Studies: http://coastalstudies.org

National Oceanic and Atmospheric Administration, Northeast Fisheries Science Center: https://www.nefsc.noaa.gov

North Atlantic Right Whale Initiative, Woods Hole Oceanographic Institution: https://www.whoi.edu/page.do?pid=96471

POLAR BEAR

Polar Bears International: https://polarbearsinternational.org

World Wildlife Fund, Polar Bears: https://www.worldwildlife.org/species/polar-bear

U.S. Geological Survey, Alaska Science Center: https://www.usgs.gov/centers/asc

LOWLAND TAPIR

Lowland Tapir Conservation Initiative: https://tapirconservation.org.br

Global Conservation Network, Global Tapir Program: https://www.globalwildlife.org/project/tapirs

The Tapir Specialist Group (of the IUCN Species Survival Commission): https://tapirs.org/about

GOLDEN RIFFLESHELL MUSSEL

Freshwater Mollusk Conservation Society: https://molluskconservation.org/index.html

Center for Mollusk Conservation: https://fw.ky.gov/Wildlife/Documents/CenterBrochure2013.pdf

Clinch-Powell Clean Rivers Initiative: http://cpcri.net

OLM

Zoological Society of London's Edge of Existence Program, the Proteus project: http://www.edgeofexistence.org/species/olm

Tular Cave Laboratory, Slovenia: https://www.tular.si/index.php/tular/5-tular-cave-lab

LAYSAN ALBATROSS

Cornell Lab of Ornithology: https://www.allaboutbirds.org/guide/Laysan_Albatross/overview

The Ocean Conservancy: https://oceanconservancy.org/wildlife-factsheet/laysan-albatross

Albatross, a film: https://www.albatrossthefilm.com

GIANT RIVER OTTER

Save the Giants: https://savethegiants.org

World Wide Fund for Nature, Guianas: http://www.wwfguianas.org

Cocha Cashu Biological Station (Peru): http://cochacashu.sandiegozooglobal.org/giant-otter-conservation-program

CHINESE PANGOLIN

International Union for the Conservation of Nature, Pangolin Specialist Group: https://www.pangolinsg.org

Zoological Society of London, Pangolin Conservation: https://www.zsl.org/conservation/how-we-work/illegal-wildlife-trade-crisis/pangolin-conservation

Save Pangolins: https://www.savepangolins.org

RING-TAILED LEMUR

Lemur Conservation Network: https://www.lemurconservationnetwork.org

Lemur Love: http://www.lemurlove.org/

Beza Mahafaly Special Reserve: https://campuspress.yale.edu/bezamahafaly/support-beza

BLACK RHINOCEROS

Save the Rhino International: https://www.savetherhino.org

International Rhino Foundation: https://rhinos.org

HAWKSBILL TURTLE

The Nature Conservancy, Sea Turtle Project: https://www.nature.org/en-us/about-us/where-we-work/asia-pacific/the-pacific-islands/stories-in-the-pacific-islands/community-partnerships

Sea Turtle Conservancy: https://conserveturtles.org/information-about-sea-turtles-hawksbill-sea-turtle

World Wildlife Fund, Sea Turtle Projects: https://www.worldwildlife.org/species/hawksbill-turtle

BONOBO

The TL2 Project of the Lukuru Foundation: http://www.bonoboincongo.com

Bonobo Conservation Initiative: www.bonobo.org

Lola Ya Bonobo Sanctuary: https://www.lolayabonobo.org

ATLANTIC BLUEFIN TUNA

Tuna Research and Conservation Center: https://www.tunaresearch.org

The Safina Center: http://safinacenter.org

Oceana: https://oceana.org/what-we-do

AFRICAN ELEPHANT

Save the Elephants: https://www.savetheelephants.org

David Sheldrick Wildlife Trust: https://www.sheldrickwildlifetrust.org

The Amboseli Trust for Elephants: https://www.elephanttrust.org

Elephant Voices: https://elephantvoices.org

TAKHI

Association for the Przewalski Horse, Takh: https://www.takh.org/en

International Takhi Group: https://www.savethewildhorse.org/en

ACKNOWLEDGMENTS

Before a word of this book was written, people were seeding it. After it was begun, many helped it grow.

Thank you, Rachelle Oppenhuizen, for handing me an article on the red knot and, though you barely knew me, having the insightful audacity to say, "This is what you should write next."

Thank you, Father Rick Lawler and Heather Young, for emailing after you'd read *All Creation Waits: The Advent Mystery of New Beginnings* and asking, "Would you consider writing a sequel, for Lent?" The idea had not occurred to me.

And to the many others who also wrote after reading *All Creation Waits*, thank you for committing to pray for this book as it slowly took shape. Your prayers sustained me for the two and a half years I was immersed in the suffering of innocents.

As with the Advent book, I'm indebted to the scientists and conservationists whose fieldwork—often under conditions that would crush most of us—supplied the raw content for this Lenten book. I stand awed and inspired by what you do.

Translating the science into short stories, I sometimes got lost in a morass of information. Thank you, Tamara Dean and Cheryl Hellner, for the loving and laser focus you gave to every word of the manuscript. You kept me on the path.

The creatures in this book are more beautiful than words alone can convey. Thank you, David Klein, for once again creating illustrations that evoke their beyond-words beauty.

Thank you to editor Jon Sweeney, managing editor Robert Edmonson, and the community at Paraclete Press for welcoming an unusual Lenten book. And for your long-distance friendship.

Many faithful family members and friends graced my life while I was writing this book. Though often you didn't see or hear from me for weeks, I felt your encouragement—spoken, emailed, prayed—and was grateful. I still am.

My sons, Kai and Cotter, planted the earliest seeds for this book nearly twenty years ago with their bored disinterest in my descriptions of Lent and their fascination with animals. I look to them still—and now also to daughter-in-law, Kellan—reading on their faces and bodies whether my words have, or lack, the animal juice of life. Thank you, beloveds.

And to Doug, the one who, for almost four decades, has held me dear: This book was only possible in the sphere of your endearment. Thank you, thank you.

ABOUT PARACLETE PRESS

Who We Are

As the publishing arm of the Community of Jesus, Paraclete Press presents a full expression of Christian belief and practice—from Catholic to Evangelical, from Protestant to Orthodox, reflecting the ecumenical charism of the Community and its dedication to sacred music, the fine arts, and the written word. We publish books, recordings, sheet music, and video/DVDs that nourish the vibrant life of the church and its people.

What We Are Doing

BOOKS | Paraclete Press books show the richness and depth of what it means to be Christian. While Benedictine spirituality is at the heart of who we are and all that we do, our books reflect the Christian experience across many cultures, time periods, and houses of worship.

We have many series, including *Paraclete Essentials*; *Paraclete Fiction*; *Paraclete Poetry*; *Paraclete Giants*; and for children and adults, *All God's Creatures*, books about animals and faith; and *San Damiano Books*, focusing on Franciscan spirituality. Others include *Voices from the Monastery* (men and women monastics writing about living a spiritual life today), *Active Prayer*, and new for young readers: *The Pope's Cat*. We also specialize in gift books for children on the occasions of Baptism and First Communion, as well as other important times in a child's life, and books that bring creativity and liveliness to any adult spiritual life.

The Mount Tabor Books series focuses on the arts and literature as well as liturgical worship and spirituality; it was created in conjunction with the Mount Tabor Ecumenical Centre for Art and Spirituality in Barga, Italy.

MUSIC | The Paraclete Recordings label represents the internationally acclaimed choir *Gloriæ Dei Cantores*, the *Gloriæ Dei Cantores Schola*, and the other instrumental artists of the *Arts Empowering Life Foundation*.

Paraclete Press is the exclusive North American distributor for the Gregorian chant recordings from St. Peter's Abbey in Solesmes, France. Paraclete also carries all of the Solesmes chant publications for Mass and the Divine Office, as well as their academic research publications.

In addition, Paraclete Press Sheet Music publishes the work of today's finest composers of sacred choral music, annually reviewing over 1,000 works and releasing between 40 and 60 works for both choir and organ.

VIDEO | Our video/DVDs offer spiritual help, healing, and biblical guidance for a broad range of life issues including grief and loss, marriage, forgiveness, facing death, understanding suicide, bullying, addictions, Alzheimer's, and Christian formation.

Learn more about us at our website
www.paracletepress.com
or phone us toll-free at 1.800.451.5006